My
SUPERCONSCIOUS
MIND

MARCAS MAJOR

Published by MP2ME Enterprise LLC
ISBN: 978-0-9841360-7-0 (Hardback)

For information, please contact:
marcasmajor@gmail.com:
marcasmajor.com

This book is dedicated to:
My loving and supportive family.

Look Within by Marcel Pighin

Contents

What lurks in the shadows, way out yonder?

I look and I ponder.

My soul yearns to wander,

Far, far away...

Marcas Major 10-31-2022

Chapter 1: Who Am I?

MY CHILDHOOD

My mom's parents originally came from Quebec. They were French Canadian, and their family tree in the Quebec area has North American roots dating back to the early sixteen hundreds. My mom's family settled in Saskatchewan for the early part of her life. Her family was forced to move westwards in the 1930s to escape a devastating drought in the Midwest during the Great Depression. The once fertile land of America's Heartland had turned into a desert—the Great Dust Bowl. Approximately three and a half million people migrated out of the Great Plains states and provinces between the 1930s and 1940s.

The family could not afford train tickets to carry out their escape. Instead, they traveled west by covered wagon. Unfortunately, their horse, Mabel, died while pulling this wagon over the rugged Rocky Mountains in British Columbia (BC), Canada.

Irma was my mom's name. Irma's parents settled near Cranbrook, BC. I assume Cranbrook was close to the location where their horse, Mabel, died pulling the covered wagon. The elevation of Cranbrook, BC is 3022 feet. The family started a new life. Irma loved animals. She honored Mabel the horse by giving one of my three sisters the middle name of Mabel. I also have an older brother, two stepsisters, and one stepbrother.

Irma married an Italian man named Walter. He was much older than her and had been previously married. His dad had migrated from the Udine area of Italy, just north of Venice. My dad's previous wife died during childbirth. She had given birth to a boy and a severely intellectually disabled girl. By the time I came along, my dad's first son, Clary, was already married and had children. Elaine, my disabled half-sister, lived with us until I completed third grade.

My dad built a whole dairy business with a pasteurizing plant, milk truck delivery, and support staff. The staff worked on billing, customer payments, and employee salaries. We were well-off compared to the greater majority of lead and zinc miners in Kimberley, BC. We moved into a larger house in Kimberley, BC. Kimberley was less than twenty miles from Cranbrook, BC.

I was only one and a half when my dad was killed by a drunk driver. My dad was driving to Creston, BC when the accident occurred. He was going there to sell some pasteurizing equipment.

In an instant, this single incident changed the course of my family's life. My mom only had a ninth-grade education. She had to sell the dairy business because she did not have enough education to understand how to run it. I found out later in life she did not even understand the concept of interest gained by placing money in a savings account. She asked me,

Why would people give you more money for letting your funds sit in a bank savings account?

It made no sense to her.

To make ends meet, my mother took on boarders who rented extra bedrooms in our large house at a time when there were many men in the city installing natural gas lines. I remember my siblings being rambunctious, back then. We yelled at each other and called each other stupid a lot. There was one gas line boarder who could not speak English at all when he first came and stayed at our house. The first English word I remember him ever saying was:

Shtupid!

My childhood memories of living in Kimberley, BC were happy ones. I started school in a kindergarten run by the nuns at the Catholic church in town. All my neighborhood friends went too. One day, when I was peacefully coloring with other children on a long Formica-covered table, a nun came by and slammed a wooden ruler between me and the boy next to me. It really scared me. Instead of cowering in fear, I yelled at the nun. I told her I had not done anything. I was just coloring. She was surprised by my sudden outburst. She quickly gained a calmer composure and told me the boy next to me was misbehaving.

It was the last day I attended kindergarten. I told my mom the nuns were mean. She never questioned my judgment. I became a kindergarten dropout.

It surprised me when I discovered I still held a small grudge against nuns even later in life. I went to Rome and visited the Vatican with my wife. We took a bus to get there. I was telling my wife I thought we needed to get off at the next stop. A sweet young lady dressed in a nun's habit noticed the fact we were English-speaking American tourists. She was excited to tell me, in English, that I was correct to get off the bus at the next stop to go to the Vatican. She then proceeded to tell me she was from the East Coast of the US and had recently been chosen to work at the Vatican as a nun. She was bursting with pride.

To my surprise, I said,

Cool, how is that gig going?

She was taken aback a little by my attitude but replied positively to my question. No respect, I know. I was sorry as soon as I said it.

I have never been enthralled with all the dogma of the Catholic Church. I only saw priests and nuns as ordinary people running a huge conglomerate business. Most Catholic nuns and priests do a wonderful job of spreading the word of eternal love and the concepts of right or wrong. Yet, I found out at an early age that some nuns and priests were not very nice people. This has since been borne out through the many lawsuits against Catholic priests — some were, indeed, capable of some very bad behavior. I have always thought there must be a better way to have a strong relationship with God without the strict rules of the various religions around the world.

I remember my younger years with fondness after my father's death. I was too young, when he died, to even remember what he looked like. Was my father's death fate? Was my choice to cease going to the Catholic kindergarten completely up to me? I am starting to believe I was truly being protected and guided by a spiritual guardian. You will see my reasons for my belief as you make your way through this book.

Compared to many other children, I was a free spirit. My mom told her kids they could be anything they wanted to be if they set their minds to it. I was allowed a lot of independence as I was growing up.

Irma became a single parent raising five children — all spaced about two years apart as well as one severely disabled young adult from my dad's previous marriage. She did not have a lot of time to do much else besides get meals ready and do housekeeping.

I believe my dad's death changed the course of my family's life for the better. My mom remarried a man who was highly trained to go from one town to the next setting up dry cleaning shops from scratch. My mom gave birth to my youngest stepsister, Diane, before we moved to the United States in 1963. I was just entering fourth grade. Four of my original family members, together with Diane, moved to Everett in Washington State.

My stepfather's reason for moving was based on simple math: the United States had many more people than Canada did, so more people in the US needed their clothes dry-cleaned to go to work every day. Back then, a woman had to wear a dress and pantyhose to work and a man had to wear a stuffy suit with a tie. Worse yet, many people still smoked cigarettes at work. The smoke stuck to their work clothes. Cigarette smoke is made up of ugly yellow tar which easily saturates clothes, so dry cleaning services were definitely in demand back then.

I struggle with a lack of concentration and a tendency to act on spontaneous impulses. After moving to the US, I was better able to channel these impulses into positive acts — most of the time. I ran into a few problems but was given the support I needed at the right time to pull me out of the emotional hole I was in. I think the key is to face the reality of your situation and then take the action needed to remedy it. I noticed successful people I met had amazing amounts of energy and worked hard for goals they wanted to achieve. So, I worked hard for goals I wanted to achieve too.

When we moved, we left Clary, my half-brother, and my disabled half-sister, Elaine, in Canada. Clary was already married in Kimberley and had children. I thought it was cruel to leave Elaine in Canada, but it turned out to be the best decision for her. She ended up on a farm for special needs adults and had a much better life than she would have had if she had come with us to the United States. She learned how to make items to sell at a yearly craft show and was free to roam around the beautiful farm nestled on Vancouver Island.

I cannot say my life growing up in the United States was easy. My mom struggled to pay the bills each month. My stepfather was a nice person but had a bit of a traveling salesman mentality, with questionable morals and little concern for paying the Internal Revenue Service (IRS) his taxes each year. He was seldom home to help raise the family. My mom learned how to run her dry cleaning shop from my stepfather. My mom was dedicated to raising her kids the best way she knew how and was very proud of her children. She also made sure the critical month-to-month bills were paid, like house mortgage payments, so we would not be thrown out on the street.

My stepfather racked up a ton of unpaid tax and business bills when setting up several dry cleaning shops in the Northwest area of the US. In the end, the IRS finally caught up with him. He ended up spending a few months in jail and was given a one-way ticket back to Vancouver, BC, Canada where he retired and passed away.

With advice from a lawyer, my mother divorced my stepfather after about twenty years of marriage to avoid having to pay all the outstanding debts he had racked up right before being escorted out of the US. The Catholic Church did not believe in divorce, so it was a difficult decision for my mother. I believe she still had to pay at least a portion of the IRS back taxes due. It took her several years to get out of debt. She worked very hard but seemed to enjoy the person-to-person relationships her dry cleaning business provided her.

Sadly, my mom's meager retirement savings were scammed away by nefarious mailings from people who convinced her she was going to be the next big winner of the next who-knows-what mail-order contest. No one ever wins those contest scams. It was just a way to make money from innocent people.

Gambling is a disease.

My mom raised the five children she gave birth to very well. My stepsister, Diane, took my now-destitute mom under her wing during her final years.

My mom may have died destitute, but she had a heart of gold: she dedicated her whole life to her children. My stepbrother, Clary, died due to liver failure induced by drinking too much. He had been warned many times if he kept drinking, he would die. He had chronic cirrhosis of the liver. My disabled stepsister died peacefully after being well cared for on the farm created for her special needs.

As I grew up, I learned lessons from the seemingly random

events shaping our family's life. I knew I wanted to get educated enough to understand the concepts of saving money, interest rates, not being swindled into giving all my money away, and learning the rules of the road so I would not be thrown in jail for tax evasion and kicked out of the country.

I became highly educated, with a Bachelor of Science degree in Fisheries Management and a Master of Business Administration degree in Finance. I also achieved several Microsoft Software certifications. I learned to listen and evaluate the best route to follow to achieve my goals in life. My goals were partially based on my parents' mistakes and my strong innate sense of right and wrong behavior.

I had a lot more freedom to go out and explore the world by myself than most of the kids I grew up with in the US. Having a strong moral compass has been a blessing throughout my life, especially when my behavior warranted course-correcting. I was able to eventually admit my errors and do what was necessary to prevent any negative fallout from recurring.

It was easy for me to avoid the rampant drug scene in the late sixties and seventies when illegal drugs were readily available to take. Taking drugs and smoking felt wrong. My adventurous spirit was channeled into other, more positive, physical activities like bike riding and various sports. Having very little money in the nineteen-seventies did not stop me from going on some bold, fun adventures by myself.

I started college at a small, reputable liberal arts college in Walla Walla, WA. I met a guy there from Orange County in Los

Angeles (LA), California. He kept bragging about all the times he went to Disneyland and what great fun it was. One day, I told him he had certainly managed to convince me to see Disneyland for myself. I asked him if I could come down to LA, stay at his house, and have him take me to Disneyland. He said, *Yes!*

Without much money to go, I said to myself, *Just do it!*

Once I get an idea in my head, I am tenacious about accomplishing the task. So I hitchhiked from Everett, WA down to LA the next summer and went to Disneyland. Luckily, I was not picked up by any bad people. One couple was driving from Portland, Oregon to a nudist colony in Big Sur just below San Francisco. The bride was not very happy with the groom for picking up a hitchhiker along the way. The groom said I did not look threatening to him at all. He gave me a ride from the middle of Oregon to San Francisco, California.

Another example of my 'free spirit' attitude was when I went and visited my cousin and other early childhood friends in Kimberley, BC, Canada. I had very little money to make the trip so I decided to hop on my yellow Suzuki 90cc trail bike, with knobby tires, and take a road trip to Kimberley. The diameter of a 90cc piston is less than two inches. My small motorbike, built to ride on dirt trails, was not a powerhouse made to travel hundreds of miles, but I went anyway.

Let's just say that my road trip was more of a shoulder trip because I spent most of the four-hundred-and-fifty-mile journey to Kimberley on the shoulder of the road going thirty-five miles an hour. Huge motorhomes would jet past me, with the drivers having a good laugh at my feeble trail bike's strained efforts to traverse steep mountain passes. I strapped a two-gallon gas tank on the back of my trail bike so I would not get stranded in the middle of a remote mountain pass.

When I finally arrived in Kimberley, I lost the only key I had to start my motorcycle. The locksmith told me there was no easy way to replicate my lost key. I did not have any money to give him to work on a complicated procedure to create a new key for me. The kind locksmith dumped a pile of used keys on the floor and let me sift through them until I found one that started my motorcycle. It took me over four hours. It was a miracle! I had fun visiting all my Canadian friends. It was worth the effort.

Until my early fifties, I never realized I had attention deficit disorder (ADD). I had a lot of problems staying on task and tended to lose things a lot. To stay on task, I had to be interested in what I was doing. The loss of many prescription eyeglasses, over the years, should have been a hint I was not able to keep my focus on things very well. Another classic ADD trait is to just go and do things on a whim of pure emotion. It can get you into a lot of trouble. Luckily, I survived without too much trouble.

One of the most memorable statements from the psychologist who diagnosed me with ADD was,

I am surprised you were able to stay out of trouble throughout the years. Many people with the extent of your condition have served jail time.

Thanks, Doc! …

ADD children tend to act without thinking first. They get in more trouble than other children their age. Take my first day of seventh-grade class. We had a new teacher, who was a rather large lady. My mind wandered when she was introducing herself to the class, so I was only half listening to what she was saying. When she said her name, I blurted out,

Walrus? ...

I thought she had said her name was Ms. Walrus. She was so mad at me. Her name was Ms. Wallace. I tried hard to do well in her class. No matter how hard I tried, though, I could never do any better than a B grade. I was on her blacklist.

Very early in life, I became street-smart. Living in a small mining town filled with tough miners and ranchers who drank and smoked way too much was a learning experience. People tended to die young. Luckily, we moved to the United States when I was nine years old. Still, my time there proved formative: I innately knew that drinking too much and smoking was not a path to a better life. This street-smart knowledge helped me avoid acting without thinking and going down the wrong path many times in my life. When I did go down the wrong path for a while, I was strong-minded enough to recognize the problem and pull out of it. I knew I needed to get more education so I didn't allow myself to get into all the personal and financial trouble I saw around me as I grew up.

I picked challenging work projects like installing and

implementing the latest and greatest computerized program systems and computer software for various business departments at Boeing and Microsoft. These projects required an understanding of the existing business process you were trying to improve. Detailed technical knowledge of how the new computerized business systems worked and how to install the new computer software was needed to validate any improvement to the existing business process after implementation.

With determination and many smart people around me to consult, I succeeded in achieving many of my ambitions and work-related goals. I became very focused on positive projects to make a better life for myself and my family. I pursued a Master of Business Administration (MBA) in Finance at night, while still working eight hours every day at Boeing.

I cleared a piece of raw land, coordinated and helped build a house on the land, sold the house eight years later, and then built another house on a lot from scratch. I could not afford the price of a new house anywhere near where I worked. I needed more room for a growing family. It was cheaper to have one built and do some of the work myself to finish the house.

I even taught courses at the University of Phoenix for three years while working forty hours a week at Microsoft, because I found teaching a great creative outlet away from the nine-to-five daily grind.

I loved to learn. I became educated in a broad range of topics through both formal education and vocational course certifications. Some of the college-level courses I have taken were in fields such as biology, chemistry, physics, advanced mathematics, philosophy, history, statistical analysis, and computer programming. I score above average in terms of math abilities. My greatest strengths, in math, are an understanding of geometry, trigonometry, and algebraic concepts. These skills have been useful to me throughout my life.

The very first job I had at Boeing was programming a vertical, five-axis computer numerical control (CNC) machine[1] to cut out complex, curved overhead bins needed above a passenger's seat in the new Boeing 747 airplane model built at the new Everett, WA plant. By referencing a paper blueprint view of an overhead bin's dimensions and contours, I could use geometry (circles and lines), trigonometry, and basic linear algebra to outline the new overhead bin part using the Fortran program language. I defined cutting planes in the Fortran program to allow a drill bit to cut out the virtually defined overhead bin at various depths on the surface of my preprogrammed cutting planes. The five-axis NC machine was able to repeatedly follow the virtual lines and circles defining the outline of the overhead bin from the cutting instructions found in the Fortran computer program I wrote and stored on the computer. Hundreds of complex, curved surface, overhead bins with pre-drilled fastener holes, over many years, were precisely created by using my stored computer program and a five-axis NC machine.

---

1   History of numerical control. (2022). In Wikipedia. https://en.wikipedia.org/w/index.php?title=History_of_numerical_control&oldid=1111638291

Was I preordained to use my innate talents to help efficiently transport millions of people around the world? Where did my innate talent for geometry, trigonometry, and algebra come from?

I learned systems analysis techniques when in the Boeing Finance department. I also learned how to write instructions in pseudo-code (if-then-else statements). It was a trail-blazing effort to analyze and document the detailed 'if-then-else' steps required to replicate the manual Boeing Accounts Payable processes. I converted many manual Accounts Payable tasks into a series of 'if-then-else' statements. A computer programmer could then convert these into computer code. The computer program replaced the manual Boeing Accounts Payable process. The lightning-fast, computerized system only required daily data entry of new invoices to maintain the new system. Once the system was fully automated, I stayed at Boeing Finance as a systems analyst, providing support to help maintain it.

Definition of Systems Analyst

A person who analyzes a complex process or operation to improve its efficiency, especially by applying a computer system.[2]

Later, I went on to become a computer database management administrator at Boeing, responsible for storing and maintaining

---

2   Definition of Systems Analyst—Search. (n.d.). Retrieved December 16, 2022, from https://www.bing.com/search?-FORM=U523DF&PC=U523&q=Definition+of+Systems+Analyst

MARCAS MAJOR

massive amounts of Accounts Payable data for future use. It certainly paid better than a systems analyst.

I also implemented an automated parts-ordering system for the very small but talented team of Boeing engineers and mechanics tasked to build one of the first government-funded wind turbines using a research grant from the US government. The prototype wind turbine designed and built by the team I was on helped determine what technology and hardware were needed to create a viable, wind-based alternative energy source for the whole country.

There were a few design and implementation issues with the wind turbine that Boeing built, however. For one thing, I could not believe they chose to make the wind turbine tower out of cast iron. When I was a kid, we had matchbox cars made out of cast iron with tiny doors you could open and close. If you opened and closed the tiny doors too many times, the cast iron would crystallize and the doors would break off. I told the lead engineer in charge it was a really bad idea to use cast iron for a wind turbine constantly being buffeted by high winds. I told him it would crack. He did not take my advice. He told me he trusted the professional engineers responsible for choosing the wind turbine casing material. Naturally, the wind turbine developed stress cracks in the cast iron casing. Boeing switched to steel towers for wind turbine builds after discovering the cracks in the cast iron tower.

Another fun fact: Once the windmill was built, they ran a few tests of the monstrous wind turbine at Goldendale, WA. There were numerous complaints from the residents of Goldendale regarding the horrible vibrations pounding their homes from underground. With each swish of the giant wind turbine blade, Goldendale residents were complaining their whole dinner table would vibrate and cause the silverware on the dinner table to eerily move around. Boeing engineers had to produce a way of dampening the transfer of these vibrations. The vibration problem was fixed by layering the concrete foundation with rubber. Implementation of modern technology requires many iterations of trial and error.

Chapter 2: Déjà vu and Ghosts

INTRODUCTION

Since I had such a broad education in many fields, I decided to use some of the knowledge and logic I had acquired to try and solve a difficult problem no one else seemed to want to deal with. For example, the proposition that déjà vu is more than just a random, familiar feeling you have when experiencing something you have never done before.

I also wanted to figure out if there was any valid scientific explanation for people who claimed to be able to talk to and see ghosts. I knew I only had a *ghost of a chance* to figure out the reason behind this phenomenon. The scientific community was not taking any interest in determining why déjà vu or ghosts exist.

Throughout my life, I have been known to figure things out (problems or puzzles) that other people in my education classes or at work could not solve. I am not saying I was the first to discover anything. All I am saying is that often, using the limited amount of knowledge I had on a subject, I was able to make the leap in logic needed to solve a problem in situations where many others around me had failed.

Persistent and consistent blogging of strange dreams, and a lot of research conducted over many years, were required to come up with positive proof of prescient déjà vu experiences and a plausible, scientific reason for visions of ghosts and clairvoyance. I collected blogs from strange dreams I had, starting in 2005, at the blog site, Religion of One (https://relofone.blogspot.com).

Creating a searchable blog of all the puzzling dreams I had was a sound, scientific way to start looking for repeatable patterns in my strange dreams and figuring out how the subconscious mind works.

I believe the subconscious mind is where my strange dreams originate. The subconscious mind has no concept of the past, present, or future. Past, present, and future visions can happen in a single dream. It seems to me this single fact may be a huge hint regarding the true nature of time.

Do past, present, and future events in our lives already exist when we are born? Are we just records replaying the songs of our life on a universal phonograph after we incarnate?

One of my mom's relatives took the time to research and document the family's ancestral history. My mom's side of the family can be traced back to a Frenchman who came to America in the early 17th Century. He was a merchant marine and established a successful cargo transport company using a whole fleet of sailing ships. He shipped furs and other supplies from Quebec to early American settlers along the East Coast. At least three of my mom's children, including myself, ended up working in the transportation business almost four hundred years later. It makes me wonder if many of my mom's children have 'transportation business' genes embedded in their DNA and we are simply playing an old song recorded in our genes because it feels like the right thing to do.

A PRESCIENT EXAMPLE OF DÉJÀ VU

I have concluded that déjà vu is not always a random coincidence. I had a dream on Wednesday, October 19, 2005, matching a real-life event that occurred two years later...

I believe there is an emotional aspect to fate. It represents signposts in your life that are emotionally charged for one reason or another. They don't occur too often but represent major crossroads or decision points in your life and shape the trajectory of the way you live after that point...

I believe my dream is one such milestone ... a real-life event in my future.

I can see myself walking on a sidewalk in a very nice black suit. In terms of my physical appearance, I have greying hair and am smiling. What I find odd about this dream is I am walking alone. I have a family. Where are they? It is also odd I was smiling in my dream.

My first assumption, given that I am wearing a black suit, is that I must be coming from a funeral. In such circumstances, it is not unusual to wear a black suit, but why am I smiling? I find the fact I am smiling disturbing. There is something emotional going on there.[3]

On Saturday, August 11th, 2007, this dream became a reality. I attended the funeral of my half-sister in Kimberley, BC, and carried her ashes to the family burial plot to be buried near my father. Elaine was much-loved in the community where she lived most of her life. She thrived in this community.

I have had no contact with my half-sister since 1962. Yet, I went to her funeral without my family this past weekend. I walked alone in a black suit to the funeral, carried her ashes out of the church service, and brought them to the graveyard for burial.[4]

On the surface, it appears life is a bunch of random experiences not fully under your control. The general belief is you must take the hand you are dealt and make the best of it.

Right?

I no longer believe life is a bunch of random events.

3   Major, M. 'I predicted the future on Wednesday, October 19, 2005', Religion of One (8-16-2007). https://relofone.blogspot. com/2007/08/i-predicted-future-on-wednesday-october.html
4   Ibid.

CONCLUSIONS REGARDING DÉJÀ VU

My prescient dream about Elaine's funeral and the real-life funeral event I attended two years later was not a random déjà vu experience. Could attendance at Elaine's funeral have been preordained at a higher level of consciousness? I knew two years earlier the color of the suit I would be wearing and the fact I would be making the trip alone, without my family. I walked down the street alone to the funeral proceedings exactly as it was in my dream two years earlier.

Déjà vu is not always just a coincidence.

After fifteen years of documenting and interpreting my dreams on the Religion of One (relofone.blogspot.com) website, I became good at interpreting cryptic messages from my subconscious mind. I started seeing recurring patterns or hints even during my waking hours. My conscious mind had expanded its scope of reality. I started to be aware of, and interpret, subtle hints from what I saw and heard around me every day during my waking hours, as well as when I was asleep in a more unconscious state of mind.

I felt compelled to interpret cryptic words, phrases, images, and occasionally recurring patterns in numbers. I was receiving these cryptic signs from random, outside stimuli and voices in my head. The voices I heard as I woke up or when I was fully awake were more easily understood than the way my subconscious mind was communicating to me in my dreams. I felt these voices were not from my subconscious mind. I suspected I was receiving spiritual guidance, even though, logically, I was not one hundred percent convinced.

SEEING GHOSTS

Below is a summary of a blog entry I wrote right after I became certain it is possible to see ghosts.

What state was I in during the early morning of 12-08-2019 when I saw ghosts?[5]

Answer:

… A state of SCHIZOPHRENIA …

At first, this explanation sounds crazy – literally.

Based on known quantum particle/wave behavior, I believe if you are in a highly sleep-deprived state (a trigger for schizophrenic behavior) you can see ghosts and it isn't your imagination running wild.

…In the early morning of 12-08-2019, I had several quick visions of ghosts. I vowed the next time I saw a ghost I would try to note what physical state I was in because it is a rare experience when I see one. I have a good idea now of what state I need to be in to see ghosts. I'll research my new ghost ideas and publish the ideas and supporting research I've done in the next book I write…

5   Major, M. 'I swear I saw a ghost!', Religion of One (02-06-2010). https://relofone.blogspot.com/2010/02/02062010-i-swear-i-saw-ghost.html

I also saw a vision of myself during the time I was seeing ghosts in my latest sleep-deprived schizophrenic state of mind. My face in these schizophrenic visions was a mass of burned scars. It shocked me. I didn't add those extremely personal visions in my original blog of 12-08-2019. I admit, now, that having these warped and burn-scarred visions of myself at the same time I was seeing ghosts was further evidence I was in a state of schizophrenia.

… I had spent most of the night and early morning the following day tweaking a painting I was working on. I can get into almost a single-minded, obsessive/compulsive state of mind when I am close to finishing a painting and want to get it done. It is an ADD behavior called hyperfocus.[6]

I was mentally exhausted with a VERY LOW ENERGY LEVEL. This is the AHA moment my logical mind picked up on. I somehow had a clue that the combination of being in a state of severe sleep deprivation and very low energy makes you vulnerable to unusual SCHIZOPHRENIA.

After thinking about it for a few days and reviewing videos on the principles of Quantum Physics, my subconscious mind said:

Of course. When your mind is in a state of extreme sleep deprivation, hence low energy, you may see ghosts made out of waves and not particles. If you can measure a wavelength, isn't it the same as 'seeing' the wave?

6   Hyperfocus and the ADHD Brain: Intense Fixation with ADD. (n.d.). Retrieved December 25, 2022, from https://www.addi-tudemag.com/understanding-adhd-hyperfocus/

Therefore, I can see 'waves' of ghosts in low-energy, sleep-deprived environments.

This is due to the Heisenberg Uncertainty or Indeterminacy Principle. Low-energy sub-atomic particles act more like waves than they do like particles. At a quantum level of sub-atomic particle existence, the longer the wavelength (lower energy waves), the easier it is to measure the velocity of the wave ... you give up knowing the location of the sub-atomic particle(s) because the particles are more like waves now ...

Our universe of atoms required a tremendous amount of energy to produce. Our atomic 'particle' existence in this universe may be rare because atoms take so much energy to produce. ...

If your subconscious mind is working at an exceptionally low quantum energy level, the ghostly visions you are seeing in your low energy state of mind are made up of waves and not particles...

Perfectly logical.

This conclusion makes sense on so many levels of what we have observed from paranormal observations by numerous people. I think most of these psychic kids out there seeing ghosts all the time are in a perpetual state of sleep deprivation. This makes them even more vulnerable to seeing ghostly entities in a low-energy wave environment. These kids need to get a night of good sleep to reduce their ability to see ghosts.

There is also a lot known about the schizophrenic state of mind. Not all forms of schizophrenia are considered bad. My mother-in-law became severely schizophrenic after undergoing intense radiation therapy to halt an aggressive form of brain cancer she had developed. The doctors treating her finally got the brain cancer to go into remission, but she was no longer the same person we once knew. She started wearing sunglasses and was sure she heard people plotting to blow up the extended care facility we placed her in so she could physically recover from her intense chemotherapy and radiation treatments.

My mother-in-law was in bad shape. What she perceived as reality was no longer what everyone else on Earth perceived as reality. It was like she was in a different world. Her cancer had already spread to other parts of her body and she died very soon afterward.

I think sleep deprivation could be a way to study wave-like, paranormal entities.

Final Thoughts

I believe the study of low-energy waves is a unique environment we have yet to explore. Low-energy waves replace sub-atomic particles in low-energy environments ...

Trees may be more intelligent than you think. There is already evidence of intelligent choices that a group of trees makes based on studies regarding the rerouting of crucial nourishment from old trees to surrounding young trees. Better yet, low-energy, background microwaves[7] in the universe may lead us to the discovery our universe is an intelligent entity because it appears that low-energy waves can be sentient. ...[8]

It took about fifteen years to reach my 2005 blogging goal of finding a perfectly logical reason why déjà vu may not just be a random coincidence of events and why some people can see and communicate with spiritual entities beyond our current three-dimensional world.

After reaching those two goals, I felt I was ready to stop my blogging efforts and move on to something else. However, I decided to continue blogging for a while longer. I am glad I did.

I figured out déjà vu was sometimes a familiar feeling caused by recognizing a previous dream. I also finally figured out a logical reason why some people can communicate with the dead. It took a lot of research into the basic concepts of Quantum Mechanics and Quantum Physics to find the answer.

There are other odd coincidences worthy of taking a closer look at. For example, I am typing this section of the book on 04-13-2021. This date is exactly sixteen months after I wrote the original blog (above) about my AHA moment.

7   Microwaves. (n.d.). VEDANTU. Retrieved December 19, 2022, from https://www.vedantu.com/physics/microwaves
8   Major, M. 'My AHA Moment Regarding Seeing Ghosts', Religion of One (12-13-2019).https://relofone.blogspot.com/2019/12/12-13-2019-my-aha-moment-regarding.html

Repeating patterns of numbers, like eleven, and repeating dates keep showing up in my blogs. I believe they represent significant milestones in my life.

Chapter 3: Spiritual Enlightenment

A FORK IN THE ROAD

As I woke up on 09-27-2020, a voice in my head said,

I sent you a message to read a book.

My logical mind responded,

I don't know the name of the book.

I knew it wasn't possible for a voice in my head to send me an email or text message …

The voice in my head clearly responded,

Journey of (the) Soul(s).

I searched on the internet and, sure enough, there was a three-book series called Journey of the Soul by Sylvia Browne. There was also a book called Journey of Souls by Michael Newton

(Ph.D.). I guess I will have to read both of them, although I thought the voice in my head was a male.

I further researched the internet to see if either author had passed away. Both authors had: Sylvia passed away on 11-20-2013; and Michael, on 09-22-2016.[9]

I downloaded Journey of Souls by Michael Newton from Amazon Kindle Unlimited and started to read it in earnest.

I found out the reasons for specific colors, like purple, in the afterlife, are clearly explained in Michael Newton's Journey of Souls book. I have documented several afterlife dreams emphasizing the color purple throughout the years of blogging. I didn't understand why I kept having these dreams.

I believed the metaphysical, philosophical realm to be so abstract I would never be able to nail down any sort of known scientific reasons for our existence.

I am proud of the fact I finally figured it out.

Yes, there is a scientific basis for intelligent entities (ghosts, and souls).

In a quantum physics world,[10] particles of matter act more like waves than distinct particles in low-energy states of existence (such as schizophrenia or different states of

9   Major, M. 'A Voice In My Head Told Me To Read A Specific Book!', *Religion of One* (09-27-2020). https://relofone.blogspot.com/2020/09/09-27-2020-voice-in-my-head-told-me-to.html
10   Uncertainty principle. (2022). In Wikipedia. https://en.wikipedia.org/w/index.php?title=Uncertainty_principle&oldid=1127501051

freezing matter). My conclusions do not conflict with existing religious ideas where we all resulted from a single source of original, all-encompassing, loving energy ... I have also concluded emotions are eternal.

We all exist from the Religion of One which is also the title of the blog I started in 2005.

Michael Newton (Ph.D.) interviewed over seven thousand people under hypnosis to try and get a detailed understanding of souls, the afterlife, reincarnation, and why we exist. He even set up an institute to teach others how to reach 'Life Between Lives' using hypnotherapy.

The Newton Institute[11] is the home of certified practitioners who provide the experience of Life Between Lives (LBL) Hypnotherapy to individuals worldwide.[12]

Reading Journey of Souls sent me on a new path. I went from concentrating on how my subconscious mind works to understanding life beyond death and my previous reincarnations using my superconscious mind. Like Michael Newton, I had to learn to be more open-minded and make an honest effort to explore subjects on the edge of true science and pseudoscience to try and understand the strange visions I was seeing in my dreams.

---

11   https://www.newtoninstitute.org
12   Major, M. 'After Being Told To Read and Starting To Read *Journey of Souls* by Michael Newton (Ph.D.) - My Gut Reaction Is OMG!!!', Religion of One (10-06-2020). https://relofone.blogspot.com/2020/10/10-0602020-after-being-told-to-read-and.html

A LEAP OF FAITH

The voice I heard on 09-27-2020 telling me to read a specific book could be considered a pseudoscientific message to some people, but I heard it so clearly in my mind that I could not ignore it. I first looked up the definitions of the words metaphysics and pseudoscience before embarking on my journey down a new fork in the road.

Definition of Metaphysics

The branch of philosophy that deals with the first principles of things, including abstract concepts such as being, knowing, substance, cause, identity, time, and space: 'They would regard the question of the initial conditions for the universe as belonging to the realm of metaphysics or religion.' [13]

Definition of Pseudoscience

Any of the various methods, theories, or systems such as astrology, psychokinesis, or clairvoyance considered as having no scientific basis. [14]

It has taken me over a year to feel comfortable writing a book on my spiritual enlightenment. I felt like the character

---

13   *Oxford Dictionaries*, https://languages.oup.com/
14   Definition pseudoscience—Search. (n.d.). Retrieved December 27, 2022, from https://www.bing.com/search?FORM=U523D-F&PC=U523&q=definition+pseudoscience.

in <u>Fiddler on the Roof</u> [15] singing the song, *Tradition*. My scientifically trained mind wanted to stick to the tradition of tried-and-true scientific facts. I did not want to fall down the rabbit hole of what I initially thought was metaphysical mayhem.

There were other strange afterlife dreams I did not have answers for (See Appendix 1).

I was finally knocked on the head one morning as I awoke and was told exactly what to read to solve my other puzzling visions of the afterlife. The 09-27-2020 message was trying to move me down a non-scientific path to give me the answers I was looking for. Michael Newton's incredible research and innovative method of hypnotherapy encouraged me to open my mind to non-scientific answers for unlocking the meaning of my strange afterlife dreams.

Here is an excerpt from <u>Journey of Souls</u>.

See Through the Eyes of the Immortal Soul

Why are you here on Earth? Where will you go after death? What will happen to you when you get there? Many books have been written about past lives, but there has been little about the ongoing existence of our souls as we await rebirth — until this startling and provocative book. When Dr. Michael Newton, a certified Master Hypnotherapist, began regressing his clients back in time

15   *Fiddler on the Roof.* (2022). In *Wikipedia.* <u>https://en.wikipedia.org/wiki/Fiddler_on_the_Roof</u>.

to access their memories of former lives, he stumbled onto a discovery of enormous proportions: It is possible to 'see' into the spirit world through the mind's eye of subjects who are in a hypnotized or superconscious state; and... clients in this altered state were able to tell him what their soul was doing between lives on Earth. What you are about to read will shake your preconceptions about death. Over many years, the author has taken hundreds of people into the spirit world. The twenty-nine cases recounted here encompass the reports of the deeply religious, the spiritually non-committed, and those in-between — all of whom displayed a remarkable consistency in the way they answered questions about the spirit world. Dr. Newton learned that the healing process of finding one's place in the spirit world was far more meaningful for his clients than describing their former lives on Earth. Journey of Souls represents many years of his research and insights to help you understand the purpose behind your life choices, and how and why your soul — and the souls of those you love — live eternally.[16]

WHAT I KNOW NOW

There is a superconscious part of our minds. There is not just a conscious and subconscious part.

Michael Newton created a procedure to explore the

16   Michael Newton, *Journey of Souls,* Llewellyn Worldwide, Kindle Edition.

superconscious mind by guiding his clients into a somnambulistic state of consciousness. His Life Between Lives (LBL) hypnotherapy technique taps into the hidden knowledge of previous lives you have lived, as well as your spiritual life after each death. Michael discovered repeatable afterlife concepts. He captured and documented LBL knowledge gained from the thousands of people he hypnotized. His book, <u>Journey of Souls</u> describes twenty-nine sample cases of LBL sessions he conducted with people through the years.

The complexity of afterlife society and the reincarnation process, from a person's afterlife to a new life on Earth, is explained in so much detail that I was frankly overwhelmed when I read the book. I kept researching all the concepts Michael Newton introduced about life after death and visions of previous lives people have lived. I could take a concept explained in the <u>Journey of Souls</u> and find other authors who talked about the same subject and came to the same conclusions.

I was also intrigued, and relieved, when Michael Newton explained why I was dreaming about certain colors having some significance in the afterlife and how your eternal soul is separated into groups with the same level of maturity as your soul, by color. In other words, the concepts Michael Newton discusses in <u>Journey of Souls</u> matched the strange concepts I had witnessed and blogged about in my dreams concerning my soul's existence in the afterlife.

All my most puzzling afterlife dreams started to make perfect sense to me after reading the books written by Newton and other reputable authors. I discovered a whole new movement of spiritual awakening by many other people around the world. Michael Newton, Dolores Cannon, Candice Sanderson, David Rippy, and many others have created a wealth of YouTube videos, as well as their published books, on spiritual enlightenment.

Dolores Cannon[17] used a method for regression back to previous lives called the Quantum Hypnosis Healing Technique (QHHT).

This technique allowed her clients to explore beyond the boundaries of our three-dimensional world. Cannon emphasized recalling a person's past lives under hypnosis, although her published books are broader in scope and describe many different subjects on the origin of humans and life after death.

People can start understanding why they are currently on Earth and what they have experienced in their past lives. They can also experience what their souls do between reincarnations and their eternal soul's ultimate goals for the future.

Cannon describes the state of hypnosis used to explore past lives and afterlives as the *somnambulistic* hypnotic state. It is a state of sleep where your mind and body are completely relaxed, yet you can walk, talk, or complete complex actions.

---

17   http://www.dolorescannon.com/metaphysical-discoveries/

Definition of Somnambulism

An abnormal condition of sleep in which motor acts (such as walking) are performed.[18]

An individual in a somnambulistic hypnotic state can appear to be awake and in control of his or her actions. However, in this hypnotic state, you become much more open to the hypnotist's suggestions. This makes it possible to have a trained therapist place you in a somnambulistic trance and send you on a superconscious journey into the past lives of your reincarnated soul or the realm of the afterlife. You can verbalize what you are visualizing when placed in a somnambulistic state of consciousness, and you can hear the hypnotist talking to you.

Everyone goes through a somnambulistic state as they wake up and fall asleep. In the somnambulistic state, you can visualize past lives and higher dimensions of existence, your soul in a previous life, or the afterlife realm of your eternal soul before you were reincarnated back to Earth. You can also verbalize what you are seeing to a therapist who can record it with a digital recorder for you to listen to later.

As I woke up on 09-27-2020, my mind naturally passed through a somnambulistic (hypnotic) state. This is when I heard the message in my head. One of my spirit guides was trying to

18   'Somnambulism', Merriam-Webster Dictionary. ¶ – Search. (n.d.). Retrieved December 26, 2022, from https://www.bing.com/search?FORM=U523DF&PC=U523&q=%E2%80%98Somnambulism%E2%80%99%2C+Merriam-Webster+Dictionary.+%C2%B6

get me to read <u>Journey of Souls</u> so I could understand all the strange afterlife dreams I kept having.

Conclusions

Michael Newton paints a very structured picture of life after death. The twenty-nine client cases he reveals in <u>Journey of Souls</u> represent a sample of repeating concepts and visions he observed across hundreds of Life Between Lives case studies. His book was the first of many other books and YouTube videos that guided me toward what appeared to be a consensus in the articles I read regarding the following metaphysical concepts I noticed in my strange dreams:

- *The meaning of colors in the afterlife*

- *The highly structured process of spiritual progression for each of our eternal souls*

- *The ultimate goal of our eternal soul's journey toward being closer to God*

- *Why several of my afterlife dreams occur on the twenty-fourth, which is the day of my birth*

- *The significance of the number eleven to me. The number eleven often appears as a standalone number. Also, I can easily derive it by adding together single digits from the date my strange dreams occur.*

- *The significance of other numbers repeatedly occurring within the dates my strange dreams happen or the dates when other significant events in my life occur.*

Several case scenes in Journey of Souls matched my strange, afterlife dreams and made me start to believe the puzzling dreams I had were actual events my soul had experienced in previous after-death occurrences.

In his book, The Immortal Soul; the Journey to Enlightenment: Case Studies of Hypnotically Regressed Subjects and their Afterlives, David Rippy describes a client under hypnosis who had a dream about an elevator in the afterlife, similar to my *10-25-2018 Dream of Ascending Into Heaven By An Elevator.*[19] Rippy's hypnosis subject was remembering a previous life-after-death experience after she had committed suicide.

DAVID: Now, where did your grandmother go? Where did she take you?

SUBJECT: It felt like we were on an elevator, but there was no elevator. And the way that time feels, it doesn't feel the same when you're moving through it. It feels like you can take one single moment or second and stretch it out, like, to half a year or something and make it longer or make it shorter. And as soon as you don't want to be there anymore, you can leave the elevator.

DAVID: So, when you went in what felt like an elevator, did the doors open in some area at some time? How did

---

19   Major, M. 'Dream of Ascending Into Heaven- By An Elevator', Religion of One (10-25-2018). https://relofone.blogspot.com/2020/10/10-0602020-after-being-told-to-read-and.html

that work? How did you know where to go? Did your grandmother take you where you needed to be?

SUBJECT: Yeah, she had my... she had my... shoulders. She was holding me. She had her arm around my shoulders.

DAVID: Oh, well that must have been pretty reassuring, wasn't it?

SUBJECT: Yeah, she told me that I needed to go and rest.

DAVID: Now, did she say goodbye to you for a while, so you could go rest?

SUBJECT: No, I went with her.

DAVID: Where did your grandmother take you to rest? ... And who were the people that helped you? Were they nice and kind? What were they like, doctors and nurses here? If we could picture a doctor or nurse today in a hospital, what were they like on the other side?

SUBJECT: They all wore purple. Like purple doctors' outfits and nurses' outfits.

DAVID: So, they were all purple?

SUBJECT: Yeah, purple. Like lilac.[20]

[Based on soul evolution colors, purple represents the highest attainable evolvement for a soul, right under the angel kingdom dimension, and GOD above that.

---

20   Rippy, David The Immortal Soul; the Journey to Enlightenment: Case Studies of Hypnotically Regressed Subjects and their Afterlives, (pp. 208-211) David Rippy. Kindle Edition.

It's understandable that highly evolved souls assist those with difficult and traumatic endings, no different than highly specialized doctors assisting patients here with psychological trauma.][21]

My afterlife dream about an elevator ascending to higher levels in heaven occurred almost three years before I was even close to understanding the meaning of colors in my dreams. Could my crystal-clear dreams be a real occurrence experienced by my soul? Michael Newton discovered souls are grouped into the same colors David Rippy defines for the various groups of souls in the afterlife.

Finally, I know specific colors in our afterlife represent how spiritually advanced a soul is. The highest level of spiritual enlightenment by a human soul is designated by the color purple. In our soul's afterlife, David Rippy states the next level above purple are angels...

Purple is considered the highest evolution of a soul. The color denotes a soul that has had many lives, passed many tests, and had 'graduated', in a sense, from Earth School or another of God's creations. All souls have a 'color', starting at white and then, in order, pink, red, orange, yellow, green, blue, indigo, and ending with purple. The colors overlap as a soul evolves, for example: a green eventually adds some blue as they evolve toward the next higher color. Similar

21   Rippy, David. The Immortal Soul; the Journey to Enlightenment: Case Studies of Hypnotically Regressed Subjects and their Afterlives (p. 210). David Rippy. Kindle Edition

to a spectrum or chakras, a soul advances through various
stages in their soul evolution, earning advancing colors as
they evolve. After eons, souls eventually attain the purple
color designation meaning they're highly evolved.[22]

I believe most people who have had out-of-body experiences in their lives keep it to themselves. Similarly, most people are not very forthcoming about their personal experiences with UFOs (Unidentified Flying Objects)/UAPs (Unidentified Aerial Phenomena).

I was determined to get smart enough, with the knowledge of what my afterlife visions were telling me, to share my new journey into the superconscious mind. I am a trained systems analyst. It is fun for me to break up a known (or unknown) process into smaller, logical pieces and determine the best way to communicate it to the people who need to understand the process themselves.

I wanted positive proof that the amazing hypnosis techniques, which Michael Newton and Dolores Cannon created to open up one's senses to the spiritual realm, really worked. I had a great desire to experience the process of being hypnotized and open up my mind to the spiritual realm.

I am still a free spirit at heart and relish the challenge of trying to understand the great mysteries of life. Although, I had to be knocked on the head before I cracked open a book in the pseudoscientific, life-after-death (metaphysical) genre.

---

22   Rippy, David. The Immortal Soul; the Journey to Enlightenment: Case Studies of Hypnotically Regressed Subjects and their Afterlives (p. 218). David Rippy. Kindle Edition.

1

Thousands of people have gone through Michael Newton's Life Between Lives (LBL) process and/or Dolores Cannon's QHHT hypnosis process to better understand their soul's purpose. Besides the thousands of documented LBL and QHHT cases revealing similar afterlife experiences, there are also written words of wisdom from enlightened beings like Jesus, Buddha, and Confucius. Their guidance can help us open our minds to the idea of eternal, higher consciousness.

I was amazed and relieved to see my dreams validated and mirrored in other people's visions when they were under hypnosis.

Here is the introduction from David Rippy's book, The Immortal Soul; the Journey to Enlightenment: Case Studies of Hypnotically Regressed Subjects and their Afterlives.

Do not believe in anything simply because you have heard it. Do not believe in anything simply because it is spoken of and rumored by many. Do not believe in anything simply because it is found written in your religious books. Do not believe in anything merely on the authority of your teachers and elders. Do not believe in traditions because they have been handed down for many generations. But after observation and analysis, when you find that anything agrees with reason and is conducive to the good and benefit of one and all, then accept it and live up to it. – Buddha[23]

The journey toward understanding our true selves is open

---

23   Ibid.

to all of us. Authors like Michael Newton, Dolores Cannon, and David Rippy have devoted a large amount of time to understanding and documenting their clients' past lives using a carefully structured process to bring them into a somnambulistic state of *superconsciousness*. These authors have helped many other people understand their eternal souls and the lives they have previously lived.

Other Notable Metaphysical Authors

Many other gurus, shamans, priests, and wise men have shared their metaphysical wisdom through the ages from Asia to the North and South American continents. There is a wealth of books written on metaphysical subjects by centuries of authors.

Other people who have authored books or posted videos on YouTube I have read or watched were a local radio announcer (Cari Palmer), a former military officer (Suzanne Giesemann), a Washington state superior court judge (Eric Z. Lucas), and Melanie Beckler. There are many more. All these people have made YouTube videos and/or written books to get the message out there on how to forge a new path toward a greater good for humanity and a deeper understanding of your immortal soul.

Well-established institutions are also devoted to exploring human consciousness. The Chopra Institute[24], Dr. Raymond Moody's works on near-death experiences (NDEs)[25], and the

---

24   'Discover Chopra: Meditation, Ayurveda, & Self Care', Deepak Chopra website, https://chopra.com/
25   Raymond Moody. (2022). In *Wikipedia*. https://en.wikipedia.org/w/index.php?title=Raymond_Moody&oldid=1127696908

Monroe Institute are examples of such institutions.

Candice Sanderson and Cari Palmer have told me they have attended classes put on by the Monroe Institute located in Faber, Virginia. According to Wikipedia, Robert Allen Monroe founded the Monroe Institute in 1985 based on some of his own out-of-body experiences (OBE) he had while experimenting with sleep learning in 1958. He created a Research and Development division in his network radio program creation company which was established in 1953.

Robert Monroe experimented with how sound waves can affect human consciousness and the human sleep state. His business morphed into the Monroe Institute. It is now dedicated to the exploration of consciousness using effective and patented Hemi-Sync sound wave technology. This special wave technology is designed to help a person reach higher states of awareness and allow them to explore a broader spectrum of their conscious mind.

Although I have not attended any of the Monroe Institute classes yet, I like their policy of no dogma or bias concerning belief systems, religion, or political or social stances. The particular sound frequency many believe gets you into the correct meditative state for exploring at a higher level of consciousness is called the theta wave.[26]

Other specialists have created online blogs and video/podcast courses in deep conscious exploration. There are many

26   Institute, A. M. (n.d.). Theta Meditation. Advanced Mind Institute. Retrieved December 26, 2022, from https://en.advanced-mind-institute.org/downloads/theta-meditation/

different types of courses offered to expand your knowledge of consciousness. Once you get the hang of listening to your spirit guides, you will discover they are providing you with a variety of validations, synchronicities, subtle voices, and hints to actions you take or questions you have on your mind.

Ask for help to answer difficult questions you are struggling with. You will receive real, valid answers from the entities within a few minutes, hours, or days.

I am getting very good at recognizing clear synchronicities and other types of validations from my spirit guides. When, in my mind, I come to a new spiritual truth of the way life really is, I often get confirmation from my spirit guides very soon afterward.

For example, I see the number eleven a lot after I take positive action toward my spiritual growth. If I ask a critical question about my spiritual enlightenment, I magically discover published articles with detailed explanations answering the critical question I had. I attribute my finding these articles so quickly to direct help from my spirit guides.

THE NEW AGE

By expanding my journey into the metaphysical realm, I have finally found solid links relating my strange and puzzling afterlife dreams to well-researched, documented paths toward spiritual enlightenment.

There is a name for this new awareness of one's soul and the soul's journey to becoming more spiritually enlightened.

It is called The New Age of Enlightenment — except it isn't new.

What enlightenment means in the New Age Movement can be gauged through editor John White's text What Is Enlightenment? Exploring the Goal of the Spiritual Path. White is an authority on consciousness exploration and related areas, having authored or edited numerous books, such as What Is Meditation? Frontiers of Consciousness, The Highest State of Consciousness, Psychic Exploration, Other Worlds, Other Universes, and Kundalini, Evolution and Enlightenment. White holds degrees from Dartmouth College and Yale University, is on the boards of several academic and New Age organizations, and is an editorial contributor to a variety of national publications.

He writes, 'So widespread is the urge to know about enlightenment that, for the first time in history, people and organizations claiming to understand it have developed into a thriving field of commerce. The Enlightenment industry is big business.... Today, Enlightenment is for everyone.' But the kind of Enlightenment White discusses is not new; it is the age-old enlightenment of Eastern religion and occultism: that people are, in their true nature, one essence with God. As noted in the introductory quote: 'Enlightenment is the realization of the truth of Being. Our native condition, our true self is Being, traditionally

47

called God....'[27]

The *New Age* movement of spiritual awakening has been acknowledged in publications by hundreds of other people around the world.

Definition of New Age

Despite its highly eclectic nature, a number of beliefs commonly found within the New Age have been identified. Theologically, the New Age typically adopts a belief in a holistic form of divinity that imbues all of the universes, including human beings themselves. There is thus a strong emphasis on the spiritual authority of the self. This is accompanied by a common belief in a wide variety of semi-divine non-human entities, such as angels and masters, with whom humans can communicate, particularly through the form of channeling.[28]

Jane Roberts was an American author who died in 1984. She wrote ten volumes of <u>The Seth Material</u> from channeling a non-physical entity named Seth. Hundreds of people from 1967 to 1975 went to hear Jane Roberts channel Seth in the classes she held.

Jane was hit by her first spiritually enlightened experience

---

27   *What is New Age Enlightenment? - JA Show Articles.* (2012, August 6). https://jashow.org/articles/what-is-new-age-enlightenment/
28   New Age. (2022). In *Wikipedia.* https://en.wikipedia.org/w/index.php?title=New_Age&oldid=1128545624

when it was least expected. She was simply working on some poetry she had written after dinner when an incredible source of energy connected to her in her mind. I was fascinated by this next quote from Chapter 1 of her book because I remember having a similar experience. This cannot be a coincidence...

Between one normal minute and the next, a fantastic avalanche of radical, new ideas burst into my head with tremendous force, as if my skull were some sort of receiving station, turned up to unbearable volume. Not only ideas came through this channel, but sensations, intensified and pulsated. I was ... connected to some incredible source of energy...

It was as if the physical world were really tissue-paper thin, hiding infinite dimensions of reality, and I was suddenly flung through the tissue paper with a huge ripping sound.[29]

Jane Roberts went on to write several more books on paranormal and metaphysical experiences, including the extensive, deep, spiritual, and philosophical conversations with the spirit guide she called Seth, who was introduced to her during her first, powerful channeling experience. Jane Roberts' influence on the New Age movement was profound.[30]

I recently went to Sedona for a couple of days after going to the Phoenix Mayo Clinic for a final, one-year checkup. The

---

29   Roberts, Jane. The Seth Material (p. 31). New Awareness Network, Inc. Kindle Edition.

30   Roberts, Jane (2022). In *Wikipedia*. https://en.wikipedia. org/w/index.php?title=Jane_Roberts&oldid=1127056673

checkup verified my extensive lower back surgery was properly healing.

Sedona is known as one of the rare locations where high-energy vortices exist that can more easily amplify your connection to the spiritual dimension. I was surprised when my *Touch the Earth Pink Jeep*[31] tour guide said a reputable psychic by the name of Jane Roberts came to Sedona and was able to sense exactly where these highly energized vortices[32] to the spiritual dimension were located.[33]

The name Seth shows up in this book a couple more times. I have a feeling it is not a coincidence, but I have not figured out the connection between Jane Robert's Seth character and the other two characters named Seth in this book.

Candice Sanderson (http://candicesanderson.com/), the author of The Reluctant Messenger books, is very in tune with the spiritual world. Candice has documented a multitude of occasions when spiritual entities gave her profound messages to digest, validate, and pass on to the rest of the world. She has created many YouTube videos I enjoyed watching with Cari Palmer and Donna Rebadow. I do not think I would be so fully engaged when watching Candice Sanderson's videos if I had not had such powerful visions during my 11-01-2020 QHHT

31   *Sedona Jeep® Tours | Tours Sell Out Fast! | Pink Jeep Tours Since 1960.* (n.d.). Retrieved December 26, 2022, from https://www.pinkadventuretours.com/tours/sedona-tours
32   Portals and vortex's. (n.d.). Retrieved December 26, 2022, from *https://nexusnewsfeed.com/article/unexplained/portals-and-vortex-s*
33   *Sedona Psychics, Readings, & Spiritual Counsel.* (n.d.). Retrieved December 26, 2022, from https://www.sedona.net/psychics

session. My QHHT session ripped me completely out of the comfort zone of strict, scientific training and sent me on a new journey to gain a greater understanding of what I now believe is a very real spiritual world.

Candice was a practicing psychologist for a public school district in Naples, Florida when this epiphany came to her while driving to work. She describes it in the Introduction to her book, The Reluctant Messenger: Tales from Beyond Belief.

In ten minutes, my life changed forever. My comfortable six decades of living became unrecognizable. Change brings different perspectives, and I soon discovered I questioned everything I knew or thought I knew, about life.[34]

I too have ripped through to another dimension just like Jane Roberts did in her book. The following dream took place just months before I embarked on my metaphysical journey and a couple of years before reading about Jane Roberts and her book The Seth Material.

01-11-2020 Another Dream of Ghosts When Overtired

In the early morning of 01-09-2020, I went to bed at around 1:30 AM. I was overtired from chronic bronchitis and painting. As soon as I closed my eyes to try and fall asleep, I experienced a vision.

---

34   Sanderson, Candice M. The Reluctant Messenger-Tales from Beyond Belief: An ordinary person's extraordinary journey into the unknown (p. 16). Clark Press. Kindle Edition.

I saw a mass of multi-colored points of light in front of me and there were multiple, loud crackling sounds, like the discharges of static that electricity makes. The noise was very loud. The mass of points of light was mainly red and blue. I opened my eyes and saw a wispy, black cloud hovering around the bedroom light/ceiling fan combination. I wasn't afraid. My logical mind kept telling me there was no harm present.

After the very loud multi-colored points of light went away, I entered a large room where a jam-packed crowd of noisy partygoers was celebrating.

I felt like I had gone through some sort of static threshold of multi-colored lights into a 'new level of existence' where everybody was happy and having a good time! I told the crowd they were making entirely too much noise for me to get to sleep.

My logical mind suggested I go get a nighttime snack. I was not going to get to sleep any time soon with all the static electricity noise and jam-packed boisterous crowd visions I was having. I went downstairs, had a nighttime snack, and successfully went back to bed for a much-needed rest.

I experienced a sudden jolt into a very unfamiliar, spiritual realm. Reading about other reputable authors sharing their own, sudden out-of-this-world experiences strengthens the case for the existence of an afterlife, in my opinion.

Chapter 4: Numerology and Astrology

HISTORY OF NUMEROLOGY

Many people believe Pythagoras to be the father of Numerology. It has been argued the real roots of numerology were established long before Pythagoras started his esoteric brotherhood in Italy. Some scholars argue that numerology originated in ancient Egypt and Babylon.[35] Pythagorean communities spread across the southern coastline of Italy (Magna Graecia).[36] The Pythagorean communities' dedication to gaining knowledge in philosophy, mathematics, metaphysical concepts, and ideas on mental and physical health have greatly influenced the advancement of modern civilizations.[37]

35   Slybu. (2020, November 1). History Of Numerology - Who Is The Father Of Numerology? | Slybu. *SLYBU - Free Numerology Reading & Angel Number Meanings.* https://slybu.com/history-nu-merology/

36   Magna Graecia. (2022). In *Wikipedia.* https://en.wikipedia.org/w/index.php?title=Magna_Graecia&oldid=1126291047

37   Woodward, Joy. A Beginner's Guide to Numerology: Decode Relationships, Maximize Opportunities, and Discover Your Destiny (pp. 4-5). Rockridge Press. Kindle Edition.

Pythagoras was a Greek philosopher and mathematician.[38] He traveled through Egypt and Babylonia before settling down to teach in Kroton during the sixth century BC. Kroton was an ancient Greek colony located in the toe area of Italy's boot. This area is the *Calabria* region of modern Italy.[39]

Babylonia straddled the Tigris and Euphrates rivers, stretching into Turkey and touching the Mediterranean on the western flanks. The Babylonian Empire once formed large swathes of what is now Iraq, Syria, and Iran. At one point, the empire even stretched into a portion of Egypt.

From what I have read, I picture Pythagoras traveling up and down the Tigris and Euphrates rivers and then venturing off into Egypt and northern India to gain as much leading-edge knowledge of his time as he could before sailing to Italy on the Mediterranean Sea to establish a secret society of learning in Kroton. The knowledge Pythagoras gained from his journeys covered many subjects such as religion, philosophy, mathematics, meditation, and even unpopular metaphysical cult practices. He extrapolated on the knowledge gained and discovered relationships between the various ideas he learned on his journeys. For example, he realized there was a mathematical relationship inherent in musical intervals. Pythagoras expanded the idea of harmonious or dissonant musical relationships to include the makeup of the universe. He believed the universe was made up of the same

---

38   Pythagoras. (2022). In *Wikipedia*. https://en.wikipedia. org/w/index.php?title=Pythagoras&oldid=1129486565
39   Pythagoreanism. (2022). In *Wikipedia*. https://en.wikipedia. org/w/index.php?title=Pythagoreanism&oldid=1128761301

vibrational relationships as musical notes.[40]

In my opinion, if we had expanded on his vibrational ideas at the beginning of our scientific discovery era and researched all the many vibrational interactions and nuances in the universe, we would be time-traveling to other places in the universe via wormholes by now.

WHY BOTHER?

I remembered a guy I knew in high school. His name was Eric Z. Lucas. He told me, at a high school reunion we attended in our early twenties, he was studying with a guru.

My Attention Deficit Disorder (ADD) prevented me from sitting down and having a deep conversation about what studying with a guru meant. I was not on any ADD medicine back then, so I was easily distracted by other people I had not seen in a few years and wanted to talk to. For some reason, his guru statement stuck in my mind for over forty years. He also said he was into Transcendental Meditation.

I did not know the definition of guru or Transcendental Meditation (TM). I still do not understand the details of how TM works because I have never tried it. For this book, I delve deeper into the history and purpose of a guru.

---

40   Musica universalis. (2022). In *Wikipedia*. https://en.wikipedia.org/w/index.php?title=Musica_universalis&oldid=1122959098

Definition of Guru

(in Hinduism and Buddhism) A spiritual teacher, especially one who imparts initiation.[41]

Each of the ten first leaders of the Sikh religion.

An influential teacher or popular expert: 'a management guru'

Definition of Transcendental Meditation

A technique for detaching oneself from anxiety and promoting harmony and self-realization by meditation, repetition of a mantra, and other yogic practices, promulgated by an international organization founded by the Indian Guru Maharishi Mahesh Yogi (c.1911–2008).

It was then that the Beatles discovered Mahesh Yogi and Transcendental Meditation.[42]

I realized I had no clue where to start on this metaphysical journey of enlightenment. I needed guidance because I was in my mid-sixties and did not want to waste a lot of time floundering around in a vast sea of metaphysical books. I knew Eric had already swum that sea before me. I thought he could tell me where to begin. I contacted him on Facebook—forty-

---

41   'Initiation or Empowerment: what is it, why it is important in Vajrayana, how it helps, when you need it, how to receive it?', *Buddha Weekly*, https://buddhaweekly.com/initiation-empower-ment-important-vajrayana-helps-need-receive/
42   Powered by <u>Oxford Languages</u>, <u>Bing Translator</u>

four years after he told me he was studying with a guru. He had moved on to become a Washington State County Superior Court judge residing in the city where we went to high school. He had graduated from Harvard Law School.

My message shocked Eric when he read it on Facebook because I asked him about his spiritual journeys at a younger age. Gurus were not something he talked to people about, especially once he became a reputable Superior Court judge.

In his early twenties, Eric traveled with a famous transcendental meditation guru for a year. The spiritual wisdom and guidance he studied originated from Asia. The books he read were based on astrology and numerology.

Both astrology and numerology are vast topics with many avenues to go down and explore. I knew the basic astrology signs you can use as a pickup line at a bar (although I would say I was fairly socially inept and would never have frequented a bar and used those pickup lines). However, I had not delved any further than reading my daily horoscope column in the newspaper. There seemed to be a fifty percent chance I could relate these predictions to something currently going on with my life. These are not very good odds, in my opinion.

I took several statistics classes in college for my Bachelor of Science (BS) degree in Fisheries Management and later, as part of my Master of Business (MBA) degree in Finance. It was important to have a success rate better than fifty percent of the time. For example, the Washington State Fisheries Management organization wanted to be able to calculate a higher than fifty percent probability of when too many salmon fish were being caught off the coast of Washington to maintain a healthy population. After graduating from college, I was sent to spend a summer in the remote town of La Push, Washington to collect counts of the total number of salmon being caught by commercial and sports fishermen. When the commercial and sports fishermen started catching too many fish (compared to historical catch rates/day and the current estimated salmon fish population) the Washington State Department of Fisheries closed the salmon fishing season down for the summer. This method has proved to be a valuable way to keep a healthy salmon fish population available for future use.

Probability is very important in quantum physics as well. Existence at the quantum level is described as the probability of being in a certain location. The quantum world gets a little weird. A quantum particle can exist in two places at one time, regardless of distance. We do not know why. It just happens and has been proven to be true several times now.[43]

I was surprised when my doctor told me they do not know how half the medicines he prescribes to patients work. They know that by repeated trials, most people with certain conditions will have a high probability of improving their sickness by taking a specific dosage of medication for a specified period of time.

I was also surprised when Eric Lucas told me numerology was a cornerstone of his spiritual training and spiritual

---

43   Quantum entanglement. (2022). In *Wikipedia*. https:// en.wikipedia.org/w/index.php?title=Quantum_entanglement&ol-did=1128101397

enlightenment. I decided to read more about numerology because I knew Eric was a bright guy. When I started to notice specific numbers everywhere, I felt it was time to open my mind up to spiritual enlightenment without really understanding how it happens. Eric Lucas believed numerology was a key component to the true understanding of who you are and why you are here on Earth.

The point I am making here is if there is a high probability of occurrence, then you do not have to have a scientific reason hammered out for why something happens. You can still believe there is a high probability of something happening without science. This revelation opened up a whole new mystical world of wonder to me. I started asking a lot of questions I would never have asked before.

My conscious mind looks for patterns everywhere. It was not hard for me to see the calculated, repeating occurrences of eleven on the dates I had strange, spiritual dreams. Why did I keep seeing the number eleven everywhere?

It was time I listened to Eric Lucas and started learning more about numerology and astrology.

It saddened me to find out a few months after I had contacted Eric Lucas that he had unexpectedly died. I did not know about his death for several weeks afterward. When I finally heard about it, I realized I had a very quick vision where Eric Lucas revealed himself to me soon after his death. I contacted his wife via Facebook messenger and explained my vision to her because it was so clear. I wanted her to know Eric was doing just fine on the other side…

> *I just realized a flash vision I had of a black man in a*
> *perfectly white suit a couple of weeks ago was not God. It*
> *was a guy I grew up with in high school. He had died on*
> *09-11-2021 and I did not know it yet. He was showing me*
> *how happy and healthy he was on the other side.*[44]

Eric wasn't wearing a suit in my vision. He had on a skintight outfit made of a lightweight, white cotton-linen fabric. It looked like what I have seen men in India wear when it is very hot outside. He looked like he could have been an accomplished guru from India.

---

44   4:19 AM, Oct 2, 2021 Twitter for iPad, https://mobile.twitter.com/search?q=%40marcasmajor%2009-11-2021&src=typed_query&f=top

NUMEROLOGY

Definition of Numerology

The pseudoscientific belief in a divine or mystical relationship between a number and one or more coinciding events. It is also the study of the numerical values of the letters in words, names, and ideas. It is often associated with the paranormal, alongside astrology, and is similar to divinatory arts.[45]

Numerology, the study of energy in numbers, is very old and began in ancient times. It is the philosophical thought that everything is created by and made up of numbers. The numbers 1-9 each have a unique energy and combine to create patterns. The universe and all things within it can be broken down into numerical patterns based on these primary numbers. These patterns determine how everything works, including us as individuals.[46]

The British mathematician, I. J. Good, states you should not just write off pseudoscientific ideas in numerology. He suggests numerological formulas led to the theories of electromagnetism, quantum mechanics, and gravitation. Concepts of yet unknown, scientific theories could

45   Numerology. (2022). In *Wikipedia*. https://en.wikipedia.org/w/index.php?title=Numerology&oldid=1127680967
46   Tunis, Sarahdawn. Angel Numbers Mastery: Everything You Need to Know About Angel Numbers and What They Mean For You (pp. 2-3). Kindle Edition.

evolve from formulas presented in numerology.[47]

One of my most puzzling and recurring types of dreams identifies the importance of numbers and the importance of generated, repeatable patterns in the month/day/year the dream occurs. When added digit by digit, from left to right, the date of the dream can be converted to a single number. You can also try adding the single digits of the date in reverse, starting with the year. If you keep seeing the same single number popping up on specific dream dates or any special event date, then the specific, repeating number is indicating spiritual guidance or hints from a strong, spiritual presence trying to get your attention and tell you something important. It sounds too convoluted and unscientific to believe, I know, but bear with me. I found out I was using the same rules as numerology does for deriving powerful meaning from recurring numbers.

The number eleven started popping up everywhere in my life. I had to find out why. It was beginning to drive me crazy. I had difficulty figuring out why recurring numbers, number patterns and specific formulas for number generation kept popping up in my real-life events, dreams, and visions I experienced.

It was my fault it took so long to figure out. I refused to investigate astrology and numerology for an answer. I never researched the important spiritual or metaphysical meaning behind specific numbers and number sequences. I thought

47   Good, I. (2007). *A Quantal Hypothesis for Hadrons and the Judging of Physical.* https://www.semanticscholar.org/paper/A-Quantal-Hypothesis-for-Hadrons-and-the-Judging-of-Good/707ad4e08f-5b219ad8560cdc79da42c44e5471ee

it would be too much of a leap of faith to jump into the pseudoscientific reasons for the repeating number elevens I kept seeing.

Then I found out the numbers one through nine each have a unique vibration and unique meanings regarding your personality and tendencies of behavior in life. The numbers 11, 22, and 33 each have a higher, more powerful vibration level, elevating their definition to Master Numbers in numerology.

By determining your unique set of numerological numbers, derived from your birth date and your name, you can get insight into your personality and your life's purpose.[48]

Honestly, I had no burning desire to try and determine my future and the best time I should do certain things based on my numerology chart. I am happy just living day-to-day and enjoying life without stressing out about the future. I am retired. Less lofty goals are better. I hear them say Canadians love their abundant number of holidays each year. I guess I've inherited this Canadian trait: Although it is fun for me to research and learn new things, I am more of a dabbler than a diehard fanatic about any one subject I learn about.

Even now, I keep seeing the number eleven, two elevens in a row, or eleven derived from significant event dates in my life. My love for research and learning new things drives me forward to understand what others have to say about the meaning of the number eleven. If you start looking at the dates of dreams and

48   Woodward, Joy. A Beginner's Guide to Numerology: Decode Relationships, Maximize Opportunities, and Discover Your Destiny (pp. 2-3,6). Rockridge Press. Kindle Edition.

significant events or visions quoted in this book, you will see repeating number elevens, twenty-twos, etc. everywhere. I find it amazing but a bit unnerving.

In numerology, the Life Path Number is determined by adding each digit of the month, day, and year of your birth together. Your Birthday Number is derived by adding the digits of your birth day only together. Birthday Master Numbers are 11, 22, and 29. People with Birthday Master Numbers are given more gifted talents to use in their life but more is expected of them and they will be challenged with greater obstacles to overcome in their life. Sounds like my mom. She was born on 12-22-1922.

People with Life Path Master Numbers of 11, 22, or 33 are also dealing with a more complex set of two or more repeating number vibrations. If you have a Master Life Path Number, you are expected to accomplish more than the average bear[49] in this lifetime. Reference the footnote to get all the details of the importance of having a Master Life Path Number.[50]

Walking through my example date of when I was told to read <u>Journey of Souls</u>, the Life Path Number is 0 + 9 + 2 + 7 + 2 + 0 + 2 + 0 = 22. You can also derive two elevens separately by adding, from left to right, 0+9+2=11, continuing with 7+2+2=11. There is <u>no scientific reason</u> for eleven being a powerful Master Number

49   *Than your average bear – Idioms by The Free Dictionary.* (n.d.). Retrieved December 29, 2022, from <u>https://idioms.thefreedictionary.com/than+your+average+bear</u>
50   Woodward, pp. 21, 33-35.

except for the fact that thousands of years of observation and analysis have confirmed it.

Since twenty-two is made up of two elevens, it tends to magnify the meaning of the vibrational power of eleven to new levels of power.[51]

Master Number 11 has a powerful connection to a higher source of wisdom. The Life Path Number of the date, when I was told to read Michael Newton's book Journey of Souls, matches Joy Woodward's meaning for a Life Path Number equal to Master Number 11. Life Path Number 11 also has a powerful connection with a higher source of wisdom. Joy Woodward tells us Life Path Number eleven has the capability of... 'channeling its knowledge and meaning from a spiritual source'.[52]

Did Jane Roberts have a Life Path Number of 11? She was very capable of channeling Seth's spirit and went on to publish ten volumes of channeling conversations with the spirit of Seth. She was born on 05-08-1929. Her Life Path Number is seven like mine.

Adding her birth date digits equals 34. You then add those two digits together to get a number from one to nine (3 + 4 = 7).

Come to think of it, I am just beginning to channel spirits, so a Life Path Number of 11 is not required to channel spirits.

51   Ibid.
52   *Master Number 11 Meaning.* (n.d.). Numerology.Com. Retrieved December 20, 2022, from https://www.numerology.com/articles/about-numerology/master-number-11/

Life Path numbers seem to be a more accurate way to describe personal traits or characteristics of a person than Birthday Numbers in numerology, from my brief analysis. I feel like someone planted the answer in Joy Woodward's numerology book I read to determine my Life Path Number before I even read it. One excerpt from her book is the reason I am writing this book. Joy Woodward states that people with Life Path Number 7 are highly intuitive but spirituality and metaphysical concepts are a great mystery to them.[53] Jane Roberts also admitted to being unaware of the spirit world and how you could speak to spirits until she started to converse with the spirit named Seth.[54]

The key to convincing me of a theory is to determine whether it has a repeatable outcome. I can easily test this Life Path calculation out on a few birth dates to convince myself there is some repeatable truth regarding what the calculated Life Path Number reveals about a person.

Numerology has the power to show you who you are in this life and when you will have the best energy levels to accomplish the goals you were destined to accomplish. All according to a Life Path number like seven. My mind is now racing to try and figure out how to better apply my inherent talents that were revealed by my Birthday Number and my Life Path Number.

My first reaction, after reading Joy Woodward's book, is that I better not mess up as I have in previous lives, especially if the

53   Woodward, Joy. A Beginner's Guide to Numerology: Decode Relationships, Maximize Opportunities, and Discover Your Destiny (p. 29). Rockridge Press. Kindle Edition.
54   Roberts, Jane. The Seth Material. New Awareness Network, Kindle Edition, (p. 2)

strange afterlife dreams I have listed in Appendix 1 of this book are a true reflection of my past lives. I am assuming the date of the initial voice in my head is a birth date of sorts, with a life of its own. The life attached to my newly enlightened birth date now needs to accomplish the tasks it was set out to do in this world. I am the key player in making this life accomplish what it is supposed to. My current life's true purpose may be to become aware enough of metaphysical concepts so I can write this book and share my brief journey into the world beyond my current, physical life on Earth. If I do not complete the tasks I was supposed to accomplish in this life, who knows how the spiritual authorities will react when I enter the afterlife again? They will probably tell me,

You took the easy way out again!

Now I am getting nervous...

Note: I sent off my final draft of this book to the editor on 11-11-2022. Is this a sign from my spiritual guides I did well?

My Birthday Number in numerology is the same as Leonardo da Vinci's. Our Birthday Number is six. Joy Woodward's Birthday Number definition for the number six does not seem to be an accurate description of my personality and behavior in this world. I have a limited understanding of Birthday Numbers. Joy Woodward explains there are variations in behavior depending on how your birthday number is derived. I am probably a variation of the standard Birthday Number *Six* explanation.[55]

The only way these date calculations can be meaningful is if you calculate them yourself because you are the only person who knows yourself intimately enough to make a judgment on whether the numerology date calculations are accurate in terms of their appraisal of what you are capable of. You must take into account variations in the derived Birthday Number to get a better grasp of how it can help you understand what all your special talents are and how to work with them to achieve your goals.

Let's calculate the Life Path number for Leonardo da Vinci's birthday. He was a powerful soul, in my opinion. I have always admired his great talent, amazing creativity, and the huge amount of energy required to create larger-than-life-sized paintings and sculptures. He should have a Master Life Path number (11, 22, or 33).

I have stayed in Amboise, France where Leonardo da Vinci spent the last years of his life and was buried. It is beautiful there. What does this random journey to Leonardo da Vinci's place of death mean in my journey through life? I have learned I do have a little talent in the art of painting.

I toured Leonardo da Vinci's estate with beautiful grounds and a castle in Amboise. The guide on the tour said when Leonardo was close to death, he confessed he felt bad about enjoying life a little too much and not painting more than he did.

55   Woodward, Joy. A Beginner's Guide to Numerology: Decode Relationships, Maximize Opportunities, and Discover Your Destiny (pp. 16-18). Rockridge Press. Kindle Edition.

He felt like he squandered his talent a little bit by not painting more.

Born: April 15, 1452

Died: May 2, 1519 (aged 67) Clos Lucé, Amboise, France[56]

Calculation of Leonardo da Vinci's Life Path Number:

$(0+4 +1+5+1+4+5+2= 22)$

Month + Day + Year = Life Path Number

His Life Path Number is 22. This is a powerful Life Path Number.[57]

Okay, I am becoming more convinced the calculation of a Birth Day and Life Path Numbers does have validity in helping a person understand their gifted talents, strengths, and weaknesses.

ANGEL NUMBERS

Angel Numbers helped me understand why my subconscious mind kept coming up with convoluted number calculations to generate the specific number *eleven* in dates. The number *eleven*, frequently, started popping up during significant events.

Note: I was permitted to use directs quotes from Sarahdawn Tunis's book, Angel Numbers Mastery: Everything You Need to Know About Angel Numbers

---

56   Leonardo da Vinci. (2022). In *Wikipedia*. https://en.wikipedia.org/w/index.php?title=Leonardo_da_Vinci&oldid=1128618849
57   Woodward, Joy. A Beginner's Guide to Numerology: Decode Relationships, Maximize Opportunities, and Discover Your Destiny (p. 20). Rockridge Press. Kindle Edition.

and What They Mean For You. I find her wise words a refreshing and revealing explanation for so many of the strange dreams and real-life encounters with repeating numbers I have had for the past few years.

It was interesting to find out that both Michael Newton and Eric Lucas died in September on the two powerful Angel Number days of eleven and twenty-two.

Eric Lucas passed away quickly, and very unexpectedly, on September 11, 2021.

Michael Newton died on September 22, 2016.

They must have both been angels sent to Earth to pour all their loving energies into extremely worthwhile causes for the good of all the people they interacted with.

Definition of Angels

The term angel, originating from the Latin word 'angelus', literally means messenger. Angels are the messengers of God. They are divine sparks of God's love sent to guide, love, protect, and deliver divine messages to all of us. When using the term God, I am referring to the Creator of all things. The Source of all energy. This Source is non-denominational and is pure love. The name is not important, it is your higher power, so you can call it whatever you are most comfortable with. There are three types of angels responsible for assisting the Earth and humanity. The guardian angels, the angels, and the archangels. Each group of angels has a certain role in life and helps us in different ways. All of them are available to call at any time. Angels are non-denominational. They exist to help all the physical creations of God. Including us, the animals, and the Earth itself. They are loving and non-judgmental beings who take great joy in helping to raise the vibrations of the Earth. While you are walking your life's path and fulfilling your life's purpose, you too, are raising the vibration of the Earth. Each time you help the planet or one of its inhabitants you are helping the angels raise the Earth's vibration. So, in turn, the angels take great joy in assisting and supporting you. Ultimately, it is a synergistic relationship of helping each other.[58]

Identifying angel numbers is as simple as noticing numbers that stand out to you. If you see a number or sequence of numbers that stand out in any way, you are receiving a message from the spiritual realm. The number may be a different color, it may be the one number in a sequence of numbers your eyes fixate on, or it may be the same number repeated in a sequence. Often it is a number that you uncannily keep seeing over and over. If any number gets your attention, stands out in any way, or makes you think 'That's odd' or 'I wonder,' you can be certain you are seeing an angel number. This number will continue to appear until it gets your attention. You may see it one time

---

58   Tunis, Sarahdawn. Angel Numbers Mastery: Everything You Need to Know About Angel Numbers and What They Mean For You (p. 4). Kindle Edition.

and realize it is an angel number or the angels may show it to you repeatedly until you get the message. Many times, the spiritual appears in threes. If you see a number 3 times within a relatively short period of time it is likely to be an angel number.[59]

The number eleven is getting my attention. I see it everywhere these days.

According to Sarahdawn Tunis, the energy of Angel Number 11 is related to the subconscious, dreams, balance, harmony, and more.[60]

The following description of number eleven's energy is engrained in many of the significant visions and words I write in the rest of this book. If you take time to look, you will see the number eleven can be derived from many of the referenced dates when I blogged about the strange, predictive dreams I have had.

The Angel Number 11 'The Doorway'

It is common for the number 11 to be depicted as a doorway. As it carries the energy of spiritual awakening. Our ability to reach spiritual enlightenment. Such as walking through a door and waking up to our spirit, no longer concerned with what the physical world says reality should be. It is not concerned with any logic or rational thoughts. It is faith. There is no need for reasoning when we lean on faith. As faith is the feeling of knowing, of believing, without

---

59   Tunis., p 16.
60   Tunis., p 163.

explanation. The angel number 11 is a direct connection to our subconscious and the inner-knowledge and desires we are not always aware of. It is the most intuitive of all the numbers. With the energy of using feeling, intuition, inspiration, and idealism without any rationality. The angel number 11 also carries the energy of creativity, self-expression, and vision. It is the side of ourselves that we allow to dream and see beyond our physical world. It is the energy of illumination, of lighting the way to different, better, and more spiritual things. The energy of psychics, mystics, clairvoyants, prophets, and all those who are not limited by our six senses or confined to the physical world is also a part of the angel number 11's energy. The angel number 11 has the energy of leading the way and paving new roads. Combined with the energy of faith, balance, and harmony. The angel number 11 is a very intense spiritual energy, and its corresponding messages are also intense. If you see this number, often you are being called to push yourself to spiritual greatness.[61]

… No matter where you are in life or along your path, the angels are letting you know that they are surrounding you with love and light. You are never alone. All you need to do is ask for their assistance and the angels will respond.

… To talk to the angels, you need to ride your elevator up as far as it will go, while your angel rides their elevator

---

61   Tunis, Sarahdawn. Angel Numbers Mastery: Everything You Need to Know About Angel Numbers and What They Mean For You (p. 163). Kindle Edition.

down as far as it will go.[62]

I blogged about a dream in 2018[63] where I felt like I was riding up an elevator to visit the highest levels of existence in my afterlife. I noticed the people who greeted me were much nicer and happier to see me than in previous afterlife dreams I have had. I must have been at a higher level of vibration than I had been in my previous afterlife dreams.

During the 2018 dream, I also remember feeling I was not quite ready to exist at this level of the afterlife because they seemed much more willing to dedicate their life to being a leader in public service and making the world a better place to live.

As mentioned, I am sure Eric Lucas made it to this higher level in the afterlife. Eric, with a lot of help and encouragement from his wife, was dedicated to public service and making the world a better place to live. He wrote a book called The Tao of Public Service: A Memoir on Seeking True Purpose explaining the reward in striving towards devoting your life to helping others. [64]

I do not consider myself to be a leader. I am more of an enabler.

Eric's future wife approached me on one of the final days of high school. She asked me in desperation to give Eric a small,

62   Tunis, pp. 163-168.
63   Major, M. 'Dream of Ascending Into Heaven- By An El-evator', *Religion of One* (10-26-2018). https://relofone.blogspot.com/2018/10/10-25-2018-dream-of-ascending-into.html
64   Lucas, Eric Z. *The Tao of Public Service: A Memoir: on Seeking True Purpose*. Balboa Press. Kindle Edition.

folded slip of paper before I left for the day. She said it was really important and if I did not do it, she would never see Eric again.

I asked, *Why me?*

She said, *Who else would do it?*

I understood why…

I have been an enabler most of my life. I have always worked in the background, paving the way for people to be the best they can be.

From the case studies I have read of QHHT and LBL clients under hypnosis, it appears each individual has a slightly different experience in the afterlife. Their afterlife visions may reflect what makes the most sense to them in this world, enabling them to easily ease into their afterlife.

A YouTube video's quote caught my eye:

Your reality is based on the tools you have on your dashboard to view reality. New dashboard tools can expand your view.[65]

I did not have very many metaphysical tools on my dashboard at the beginning of my quest to try and understand a greater reality that exists beyond our physical world. I have more now. Candice Sanderson and Donna Rebadow have provided the referenced videos detailing some tools to add to

---

[65] *George Knapp Λ Colm Kelleher on Skinwalker Ranch, Evidence for UFOs, and the Hitchhiker Effect – YouTube.* (n.d.). Retrieved December 21, 2022, from https://www.youtube.com/watch?v=RFGMdp-4fRog

your metaphysical exploration dashboard.[66],[67]

Spirit guides kept pushing me to understand the importance of recurring numeric values I kept seeing. Numerology and astrology practices acknowledge repeating numbers are important tools to use to help you through life.

NUMBERS ARE POWERFUL

Joy Woodward advises that there are no special psychic, intuitive, or clairvoyant talents needed for numerology to be a useful tool for you. She argues that the more you embrace and use numerology, the easier it gets to recognize the times in your everyday life when it would be best to apply the talents you were born with according to what your numerology numbers have revealed about your personality type and talents. Applying numerology principles should help you move through life with more confidence because you know who you are and what you can do.[68] Seeing the same numbers over and over again are nudges from your spirit guides to encourage you towards a more productive and spiritual life.

It took a virtual knock on the head to get me to look into astrology and numerology for answers to why I am seeing the

66   The Reluctant Messenger Unleashed (Director). (2022, January 22). *The Reluctant Messenger Unleashed Bonus Episode Part 1: Tools from The Reluctant Messenger*. https://www.youtube.com/watch?v=i-kStPMhPA0
67   The Reluctant Messenger Unleashed (Director). (2022, January 31). *The Reluctant Messenger Unleashed FINAL Episode #26*. https://www.youtube.com/watch?v=VgPYMNJFhvk
68   Woodward, p 7.

number eleven so much. The first wake-up call was when I heard the voice in my head telling me to read a specific book. The second knock on the head happened when I had a virtual Zoom meeting with Eric Lucas. He surprised me by saying his metaphysical training was deeply rooted in numerology and astrology. The meaning behind specific numbers is a cornerstone in numerology and astrology to build a better understanding of who you are and why you are here.

I was still having a problem with the logic behind pseudoscientific explanations for strange dreams I had. Eric's admission of his deeply rooted ties to numerology and astrology helped me put in the effort to research the metaphysical reasons for my strange, afterlife-related dreams. It wasn't too hard to let go of my preconceived ideas. I only needed to read and absorb what the books on numerology and astrology had to say to gain a better understanding of my afterlife-related dreams.

OTHER POWERFUL CAPABILITIES OF NUMBERS

I have acquired a basic understanding of imaginary and complex numbers because I was told they were important in a dream. Imaginary numbers are made-up numbers. They follow different rules that allow the creation of formulas in math to replicate repeatable, spatial patterns found in nature. It begs the question of whether we have covered all the angles of reality. Current physics principles cannot explain how everything that is going on around us occurs.

11-09-2021 Imaginary Numbers Are Important

… *This morning I woke up and had this persistent message in my head reminding me to look up the meaning of imaginary numbers. I have learned not to ignore such strong messages from what I believe now are my spirit guides who are responsible for guiding my eternal soul toward a closer relationship with God.*

I don't even know what imaginary numbers are and why I would get a persistent message in my head as I woke up on the morning of 11-09-2021. Even the date I had the strong, persistent message on is a hint, with multiple occurrences of eleven in the date, to pay attention to what the dream is telling you.

…I looked up the definition of imaginary numbers.

Imaginary numbers result in negative values when normal number logic would say this is not possible. We have made it possible for a product of two negative numbers to equal a negative number. The value of i^2 is -1. The square of an imaginary number bi is $-b^2$. For example, 5i is an imaginary number, and its square is -25.[69]

Imaginary numbers are not imaginary.

Imaginary numbers were once thought to be impossible, and so they were called imaginary to make fun of them.

---

69   Imaginary Numbers. (n.d.). Retrieved December 19, 2022, from https://www.mathsisfun.com/numbers/imaginary-numbers.html

But then people researched them more and discovered they were useful and important because they filled a gap in mathematics... but the 'imaginary' name has stuck.

And that is also how the name 'real numbers' came about (real is not imaginary). Imaginary numbers are useful.... Science, Quantum Mechanics, and Relativity use complex numbers.[70] Complex numbers are part imaginary numbers and part real numbers.

My dream was telling me that sometimes it is best to imagine how something might be based on new rules we do not believe are currently possible in our universe. It is the same idea I discussed when explaining numerology-based formulas. Adding all the numbers together of your birth date, to get your Life Path Number, has proven to be useful to many people for hundreds of years.

Imaginary numbers require new, unconventional rules and logic. Physicists use imaginary numbers in mathematical formulas to replicate recurring patterns in nature.

The emotional and spiritual power of specific numbers is based on ancient numerology principles. Numerology has also identified recurring, numeric patterns that scientists eventually validated and used to represent specific behaviors of different forms of energy in our universe.

Follow your gut feeling and try to understand the reasons

70   Major, M. 'Imaginary Numbers Are Important', Religion of One (11-09-2021). https://relofone.blogspot.com/2021/11/11-09-2021-imaginary-numbers-are.html

for the specific numbers you keep noticing- even if you think it is silly and strange. If you keep seeing the same number everywhere, chances are other people have experienced the same strange, repeating vision of specific numbers you have.

They have already done a ton of research and documented the known reasons for suddenly noticing the same number over and over again. I now know my spirit guides and guardian angels are trying to tell me something important when I see elevens and twenty-twos.

ASTROLOGY

There is a common theme related to the number eleven from what I have researched. The number eleven is correlated to higher vibrational energy used to make each of us spiritually better and the world a better place to live. Some people believe we entered the Age of Aquarius at the start of 2021.[71] There is still a lot of discussion on whether we are in the Age of Aquarius. Aquarius happens to be the eleventh sign of the zodiac.

The zodiac is a belt-shaped region of the sky that extends approximately 8° north or south (as measured in celestial latitude) of the ecliptic, the apparent path of the Sun across the celestial sphere...

In Western astrology, and formerly astronomy, the

---

71   *EarthSky | When will the Age of Aquarius begin?* (n.d.). Retrieved December 26, 2022, from https://earthsky.org/human-world/when-will-the-age-of-aquarius-begin/

zodiac is divided into twelve signs, each occupying 30°
of celestial longitude and roughly corresponding to the
star constellations: Aries, Taurus, Gemini, Cancer, Leo,
Virgo, Libra, Scorpio, Sagittarius, Capricorn, Aquarius,
and Pisces.[72]

Aquarius is the Eleventh Sign of the Zodiac

The birth date range for Aquarius, in astrology, is
January 20th to February 18th.[73]

Your astrological sign can change at some point in
your life due to a shift in astrological dates for each
astrological sign. I found an article that explains this
anomaly.[74]

… Aquarians are the perfect representatives for the
Age of Aquarius. Those born under this horoscope sign
have the social conscience needed to carry us into the
new millennium. Those of the Aquarius zodiac sign are
humanitarian, philanthropic, and keenly interested in
making the world a better place. Along those lines, they'd
like to make the world work better, which is why they focus
much of their energy on our social institutions and how
they work (or don't work).

72   Age of Aquarius. (2022). In *Wikipedia*. https://en.wikipedia.
org/w/index.php?title=Age_of_Aquarius&oldid=1127795382
73   '*Aquarius Dates: January 20-February 18 | Astrostyle.com*. (2016,
August 16). https://astrostyle.com/astrology/aquarius-dates/
74   *Your Zodiac Sign Actually Changes Every 30 Years*. (2019, June
26). Women's Health. https://www.womenshealthmag.com/life/
a28172986/zodiac-signs-change/

Aquarians are visionaries, progressive souls who love to spend time thinking about how things can be better. They are also quick to engage others in this process, which is why they have so many friends and acquaintances. Making the world a better place is a collaborative effort for Aquarians.[75]

What is the Age of Aquarius and Pisces?

... the Age of Aquarius follows the Age of Pisces. The approximate 2,160 years for each age corresponds to the average time it takes for the vernal equinox to move from one constellation of the zodiac into the next.[76]

According to the astrologer, Adama Sesay,

[In the Age of Aquarius,] *the power is turning over to the individual, and giving the freedom for you to choose your reality based on what aligns with your soul.*[77]

My understanding of astrology is very limited. From what I do know, it appears astrology is all about cycles... cycles of the stars, cycles of the moon, and cycles of the year. These cycles affect your behavior and where you should apply your energies with the greatest efficiency during specific astrological cycles to

75   Stapleton, D. (n.d.). *Aquarius Zodiac Sign: Characteristics, Dates, & More | Astrology.com*. Retrieved December 21, 2022, from https://www.astrology.com/zodiac-signs/aquarius.
76   Age of Aquarius. (2022). In *Wikipedia*. https://en.wikipedia.org/w/index.php?title=Age_of_Aquarius&oldid=1127795382
77   2021 Heralds the New Age of Aquarius—Here's What 5 Astrologers Want You To Know About It. (2020, December 17). Well+Good. https://www.wellandgood.com/what-is-age-aquarius/

get the most out of life.

I find numerology far more powerful. Numerology is all about the power of various forms of vibrational energy within you and around you.

ALIENS, VIBRATIONS, AND FREQUENCIES

Reputable scientists are slowly becoming more open to ideas of the expanded capabilities of the mind. Mind-to-mind transfer of ideas and thoughts without any verbal communication with other people may be possible.[78]

There is one billionaire who has spent a lot of his own money, as well as US government funds, to hire reputable scientists for research into strange phenomena found worldwide and at Skinwalker Ranch in Utah. He has revealed some of the strange, unsettling effects on a person's mind and the strange, alien visions several of the people he hired have observed, even when they were not at Skinwalker Ranch.

Robert Bigelow was the previous owner of Skinwalker Ranch. He purchased the 512-acre plot of land because he was fascinated by the history of UFOs and visions of strange and vicious animals popping up on the property out of nowhere. The Skinwalker legend of humans changing into vicious animals

---

78   *Vibration And Frequency Are Different | Shift Frequency.* (2022, August 23). https://shiftfrequency.com/frequency-vibration-differ-ent/

and back again into human form originates from native Indian tribes in the southwestern United States.

Robert Bigelow obtained US government funding in 2008 to hire several scientists with sophisticated research equipment to study strange activity and sightings on Skinwalker Ranch. Robert Bigelow wanted to capture and study the paranormal and out-of-this-world (UFO) behavior on the ranch. Government-funded research on Skinwalker Ranch stopped in 2011.

Brandon Fugal bought Skinwalker Ranch in 2016 from Robert Bigelow. Brandon Fugal decided to go public with his efforts to continue scientific observations and research on Skinwalker Ranch. Robert Bigelow admitted feeling frustrated by the lack of solid conclusions as to what exactly they witnessed on Skinwalker Ranch. At times, he felt like there were highly advanced, alien beings on the ranch toying with his researchers using unknown technologies we still do not understand.

There is currently a Skinwalker Ranch TV series. It started a third season in May of 2022. Capturing all types of anomalous data behavior, vibrations, lights, and bizarre entities occurring on Skinwalker Ranch has been interesting to watch. The strange activity looks dangerous to me. The ranch is closed off to public tours because of the high radiation and vicious cattle mutilations that periodically occur. Current research at Skinwalker Ranch has also recognized the possibility of interdimensional travel and mind-to-mind communication over great distances.

If there are truly aliens flying above the ground and vibrating the Earth and animals below, then perhaps aliens have more advanced knowledge of vibrational patterns and take advantage of the various powers of vibrational patterns to do amazing things.

Even though the Skinwalker Ranch government studies were inconclusive, they ended up providing a whole new set of vocabulary to describe what could be happening here. Words like interplanetary travel of alien beings, exotic, unknown metals, direct mind-to-mind communication with alien beings, high doses of radiation exposure, physical changes to the brains of people encountering strange phenomena on Skinwalker Ranch, and interdimensional travel by UFOs.[79]

Robert Bigelow's latest effort is to look into the possibility of life after death. In June 2020, Bigelow founded the Bigelow Institute for Consciousness Studies to support investigations into life after death. He recently awarded a few winners of an essay contest over a million dollars in funds to help these people continue their work in researching and publishing their findings regarding the possibilities of life after death.

The following blog entry suggests the idea that vibrations are key to understanding how the universe really works. Historical records show us there has always been a thread of higher, unifying, vibrational forces governing even the most alien worlds in the universe.

---

79   Collins, C. (n.d.). *The Pentagon-funded Paranormal Research at Skinwalker Ranch*. Retrieved December 29, 2022, from https://www.blueblurrylines.com/2020/04/the-pentagon-funded-paranormal-research.html

06-07-2020 My Latest Thoughts Regarding 'The Secret of Skinwalker Ranch' Series on the History Channel

The last episode of the <u>Secret of Skinwalker Ranch</u> series on the History Channel was just a summary of the four episodes before. They have started thinking maybe the UFO entities are trying to communicate with them. I also noticed the summary meeting for the last episode was on September 23rd, 2019. It is amazing to me they picked a date right at the heart of the most predictive dreams of actual future events I experience.

I have been watching some other enlightening philosophical and fundamental physics shows. One show I watched introduced the idea that both scientists and mystics believe the most fundamental property of life in the universe is simply vibration. Everything in the universe we are aware of is just a series of energy frequencies at the most fundamental level of existence. Our brains are good at recognizing patterns of vibrational energy and filtering out patterns and possibly vibrations not beneficial to our physical bodies. There are also standard, repeatable patterns of energy flows in nature used by our bodies and our minds, such as the branching tree pattern of our veins and Fibonacci-based spiral patterns.

Recognizing the useful patterns... generated from vibrating energy is what is needed to advance our civilization to a *point where the aliens on Skinwalker Ranch could already be.*

The team at Skinwalker Ranch noticed excessively high levels of gamma waves, measured in Hertz with a trimeter, bombarding certain parts of the ranch. These excessive rays (or vibrations) seem to happen at the same time other odd events occur. Some examples of high gamma wave detection are when there are sightings of UFOs, shockingly excessive ground vibrations occur when digging holes in the ground, and at the same time cows suddenly die on the ranch.

If the excessive [vibrational] wave activity is coming from a source in space and controlled by a more advanced alien race, I can't help but speculate what the excessive gamma wave activity might mean. It may be very dangerous to be poking around within a field of rays controlled by an advanced alien race.

Some quick questions I came up with - some not so serious.

What if an advanced alien race has figured out a way to manipulate time and space by first isolating a portion of Skinwalker Ranch within a high-energy bubble of ALL known frequencies in the radio/light spectrum? The parabolic formations found in the earth may disperse the high energy from space to form a high energy bubble on a portion of the ranch when a portal is needed by the aliens to travel to and from Earth. What if this high energy bubble, of all existing wavelengths, creates negative energy to propel objects to other parts of the universe and back at warp drive speed using this portal on Earth? What if the mysterious large tumor appearing on one of the ranch staff members is caused by negative energy starting to pull the ranchman's head out into space, using the negative energy created in the high-level energy bubble by aliens on a portion of the ranch?

These aliens may be creating their high-energy bubble on the Skinwalker Ranch to allow for the manipulation of time and space and for creating the negative energy needed to create a warp drive portal!

Update 06/12/2020: I wonder if there is some other-worldly, metal object buried on Skinwalker Ranch somewhere. My logical mind came up with the idea if you had a metal from outer space sensitive to vibrations from the act of digging, for example, it might explain some of the weird, earthshaking, radiation-creating symptoms they are seeing on Skinwalker Ranch. Some chemicals are sensitive to vibrations such as nitroglycerin and can result in explosions or other unexpected behavior.[80]

I already mentioned a blog I wrote about going through a

---

80   Major, M. 'My Latest Thoughts Regarding *The Secret of Skinwalker Ranch* Series on the History Channel' *Religion of One* (06-07-2020).
https://relofone.blogspot.com/2020/06/06-07-2020-my-latest-thoughts-on-secret.html

wall of static electricity to enter into another dimension.[81] As of 07-10-2022, the team of researchers and scientists at Skinwalker Ranch did find a strange, large metal object deep in the mesa. The team also discovered a strange bubble-like field deflecting the path of small rockets and preventing the rockets from entering the energy bubble.

Some fractal patterns found in nature can be replicated using complex numbers. Complex numbers are made up of one part real number and one part imaginary number. Fractals also are used to create repeating patterns like the Mandelbrot set. This is a huge hint nature is using a force or dimension in the universe we do not fully understand that does not follow the standard rules for mathematic formula creation and computation.[82] Maybe frequencies or vibrations are fractal but we have not proven it yet.

There is now an effort being made toward understanding how aliens can use just their minds to control alien spacecraft. It is a realization that the theories of consciousness must be developed further to try and understand how aliens can communicate with us telepathically, paralyze our human bodies, and even read our minds.

---

81   Major, M. 'Static Electricity Wall/Gateway To Parallel Worlds?', *Religion of One* (06-30-2021). https://relofone.blogspot.com/2021/06/06-30-2021-static-electricity.html
82   *Fractals Generated by Complex Numbers | Mathematics for the Liberal Arts.* (n.d.). Retrieved December 26, 2022, from https://courses.lumenlearning.com/wmopen-mathforliberalarts/chapter/introduction-fractals-generated-by-complex-numbers/

Special frequencies may be used by aliens for various purposes.[83]

The James Webb Telescope

As of 11-06-2022, the James Webb telescope has sent back a myriad of images published at 'webbtelescope.org' for the public to review and even download. I have become a little obsessed lately looking for alien objects in space. The James Webb telescope captures a certain range of infrared light in its images. This allows digital images of the universe to be taken up to thirteen billion light-years away.

What do the incredibly detailed images from the James Webb telescope reveal about the possible existence of intelligent life in gas nebulae and galaxies billions of light years away from us?

My review of images coming from the James Webb telescope at webbtelescope.org seemed to show advanced, alien structures floating in space around gas nebulae billions of light years from us. If I am right about what I believe I am seeing, there are tons of very advanced civilizations, not on Earth-like planets, but floating in and around gas nebulae in deep space.

I have tweeted many screen prints of James Webb telescope images at https://twitter.com/MajorCirca and used photo filters to show what I believe to be many alien structures floating in or around gas nebula

---

83   Casteel, S. (2012, October 22). The Disturbing World Of Alien Abduction And Mind Control. *UFO Digest*. https://www.ufodigest. com/article/the-disturbing-world-of-alien-abduction-and-mind-control/

millions and billions of light years away from us.[84]

Dreams of Alien Objects in Strange Worlds

The 24th day of each month is around the time I have my most significant dreams and visions while sleeping and waking up. If I have a strange, memorable dream on the day of my birth, each month; many times, it ends up predicting future events in my life I have yet to experience.

Did I foresee the power of using infrared light to see objects in the universe we could never see before?

My dreams around the twenty-fourth day of each month have foretold many things before they happen. These repeatable patterns have opened my mind up to a broader spectrum of possibilities and ways of seeing and understanding the greater reality of our existence.

The following strange, alien dreams I have had are not in a spiritual dimension. They even go beyond the boundaries of the infrared-seeking James Webb Telescope images. Are there other dimensions of reality we do not know of yet where dark is light and light is dark?

3-23-2009 Existence on the Dark Side?

What if there is a parallel universe made up of mostly dark matter?

84   Marcas Major- circa 1975 (@MarcasMajor) / Twitter. (n.d.). Twitter. Retrieved December 19, 2022, from https://twitter.com/ MajorCirca

What if dark is light and light is dark in that parallel universe?

What if the living species were black as night but with the same features as species on this Earth?

What if the only way to see them is by reaching inside ourselves (inside our subconscious mind which transcends our physical universe)?

That is what I saw in a dream: The existence of an elephant-like species, dark as night, but as close to me as the nose on my face.

Weird, huh?

10-24-2013 More Views of a Dark Matter Parallel Universe?

I had a dream on 10/24/2013. I've had similar dreams before. It is a view of life in a dark world – maybe a dark matter parallel universe...?

I keep having dreams of dark black creatures [I see in my dreams] at extremely close range. The close-up view was of a flat, black piece of leathery skin with several small black eyes in it. Again, the texture of the skin was similar to an elephant's hide but totally black. This time there was a twist. I was able to view this dark world in my dream a little better by using a low-voltage, red laser spotlight.

My mind turned on this quarter-sized, low-voltage

spotlight so I could better view the details of the eyes and skin of this seemingly parallel world to ours. My view was of a series of black eyes on leathery black skin with no real body formation. I did notice that when my red spotlight hit each eye, it would immediately close as if it wasn't used to light at all. As soon as my red spotlight passed the eye(s), they immediately opened again.

In the previous dream I had, the black life forms had larger black eyes (all black pupils with no surrounding eye color). These dark creatures also had black eyelashes and a short, black elephant-like snout. In this dream, the eyes were smaller and more reptilian-like. There was not much more detail beyond that of eyes and skin on a flat plane.

Weird!

Maybe my dream offers a hint in terms of a way to view this dark, parallel universe. All you need to do is use a low-voltage, red laser light to view this dark parallel universe in detail!

11-10-2016 Predictive Dream About Seeing Dark Entities Using a Red Light Becomes a Reality

I just watched a PBS documentary last night, on 11-09-2016 called 'Treasures of the Earth: Metals'.[85]

---

85   *Treasures of the Earth.* (n.d.). Retrieved December 26, 2022, from https://www.pbs.org/wgbh/nova/series/treasures-of-the-earth/

One segment explained how scientists are working on the Hubble 2 satellite they will launch into space in 2018, to get greater clarity of objects at the distant edge of our universe. Gold happens to reflect the complete heat signature of an infrared object ... whereas other metals cannot. To accurately reflect the heat signatures of objects at the edge of our universe, scientists will coat all the Hubble 2 telescope's mirrors with a small amount of gold (two ounces). These facts from the PBS Nova episode match keywords and phrases from my prediction I posted in this blog on 10-24-2013 regarding the use of low voltage, red (or more accurately infrared) light to see dark, living entities in another world or dimension of our universe. I also noticed the date my predictive dream became a reality was about one-half of the date I had the dream. In other words, I had a dream about seeing dark entities by using a low-voltage, red light around the 10th of November and I had a dream about two dark entities on March 23rd, 2009, and October 24th, 2013!

The quest to understand our universe and why we are here on Earth began thousands of years ago. My journey takes me across the boundaries of cultures, religions, time, and space.

It is my journey. You may travel on a different road than mine but, for now, I invite you to travel along with me in the next few chapters, as I delve into a complex spiritual world to see what I can see.

Chapter 5: My Spiritual Journey Begins

THE QUANTUM HEALING HYPNOSIS TECHNIQUE (QHHT)

After Eric Lucas died, I still needed a teacher with a deeper understanding of the vast ocean of spiritual topics I was trying to navigate through. It was exciting to find out there were a few formal, proven methods of navigating through the spiritual realm.

Michael Newton's *Life Between Lives (LBL)* wasn't the only method that provided a relatively simple and safe way to journey through the hidden ocean of spiritual knowledge using my superconscious mind.

Dolores Cannon developed and perfected her unique method of hypnosis, the Quantum Healing Hypnosis Technique (QHHT), over several decades and thousands of QHHT sessions. QHHT achieves the deepest level of hypnosis possible, the somnambulistic level of trance. The somnambulistic state is ordinarily experienced two times a day: just before becoming awake and just before falling asleep. Most hypnotists do not work at the somnambulistic level, either because they cannot access this level of trance, or they are weary of working in the most mysterious level of hypnosis, which can produce unexpected results, such as reliving a past life. Dolores Cannon's curiosity and fearlessness about the unknown and untried have ensured her enduring legacy as a pioneer in past life regression who continues to pave the way for QHHT Practitioners now and in the future with her QHHT classes.

Dolores Cannon began her research of sacred knowledge and reincarnation nearly 50 years ago by fine-tuning her QHHT method of hypnosis. By creating a safe and effective method for bypassing the chatter of the conscious mind and focusing on obtaining unlimited information in the Somnambulistic state, Dolores Cannon discovered time travel is possible at any time or place to relive one's past lives.

QHHT is a powerful tool to access that all-knowing part of us we call the Higher Self, the Oversoul; even the Soul itself. When we incarnate on Earth, we forget our previous lives and connection to our souls and The Source. QHHT enables all people from any background, culture, religion, or belief system to engage with what she called the Subconscious since it resides beyond the conscious mind. Dolores's term the Subconscious, which she later abbreviated to the SC, is that greater part of ourselves that is always connected to The Source, or God, and has unlimited knowledge and an endless ability to heal the physical body. Sometimes mental and physical ailments are rooted in trauma from past lives; sometimes they are connected to lessons being learned in a person's present life. The SC reveals the cause and will assist according to any soul's particular lessons.

By helping thousands of people relive their past lives and heal themselves by using QHHT, Dolores Cannon discovered a treasure trove of lost knowledge and insights she shared as an author of 19 extraordinary books which cover a myriad of metaphysical concepts and feature historical figures such as Jesus and Nostradamus, as well as Extraterrestrials, UFOs, the origins of life, and The Source of all creation.

... Dolores Cannon's Level 1 QHHT class, which features videos of Dolores, is available to take online currently in English, Spanish, Chinese, and Russian. And Dolores's daughter Julia Cannon will continue the tradition of teaching Level 2 and the new Level 3 QHHT classes in person in Arkansas and all over the world.[86]

It was not easy finding a QHHT or LBL (Life Between Lives) therapist in my area. I finally asked another reputable psychic whom she would recommend. She gave me the name of a QHHT therapist she thought was wonderful. She said I would

86   Dolores Cannon's QHHT Official Website, https://www.qhhtofficial.com/about-us; QHHT History - St. George Hypnosis Center, https://stgeorgehypnosiscenter.com/qhht-history/

be very happy with the results of her QHHT session. Her name was Alannah.[87]

Alannah was listed on the official QHHT website as a valid QHHT therapist, with the second of three levels of training in QHHT.[88]

I had unbound enthusiasm to quickly jump into a QHHT session. Apart from knowing what soul meant, at the time of booking a local QHHT session, I was almost completely ignorant of the unique meanings of most of the metaphysical vocabulary needed to understand the powerful visions I had during my session. My ignorance did not stop me from jumping right in to see what I could see. Alannah told me I could research what I did not understand by listening to the digital recordings of my session afterward. I did not know my QHHT visions would have such complex meanings and span thousands of years of history.

Dolores Cannon explains that the hypnosis technique she perfected is more like a vivid daydream you experience and can describe to your QHHT therapist while you are in an altered state of mind. These descriptions are digitally recorded by the QHHT therapist during your therapy session. When the session is complete, an email is sent to you with the recordings attached for future review.

---

87   Alannah permitted me to use her name in this book.
88   Alannah MCKEEHAN. (n.d.). Alannah MCKEEHAN. Retrieved December 21, 2022, from *http://qhhtselfhealing.weebly.com/*.

PRE-QHHT PRACTICE EXERCISES

About two weeks before my actual QHHT session, Alannah sent me some exercises on how to reach a calm, relaxed state of mind and imagine different scenes in my mind. An example of such an exercise would be something like this:

You arrive at a rustic cabin in the woods. The door is slightly open. Walking into the cabin, you find a fire going in a large stone fireplace covered with soot. There is a wooden chair on the floor flipped over onto its back as if someone had just left in haste. Imagine this scene in your mind. What happens next? Just let your mind flow through the house and wherever it wants to go. Do not judge or stop the scene from playing out in your mind. Just let your thoughts flow.[89]

This method of imagining very specific scenes in your mind opens up a higher level of consciousness. Your mind is free to flow where it wants to go without the limitations of conscious thought interfering through fear, criticism, or expectations. It teaches your mind to flow freely.

I have never had any practice exercises like this before in my life. I dutifully practiced the homework. I set my mind free and learned how to get in the right frame of mind to start seeing images without judging whether they made any sense or not.

In one practice session, I had a vision of a strange-looking

89   candacecrawgoldman. (2013, January 19). Feeding Your Imaginative Self. *Candace Craw-Goldman*. https://candacecrawgoldman.com/feeding-your-imaginative-self/

man on a park bench. He was a rather short, stocky person with a huge, square-shaped head. He wore a very old, deep-red, velvet, smoking jacket. He said, *Remember the word velvet.*

My mind tried to judge this strange vision. I needed to stop judging the visions I saw in my practice sessions. This whole mind-freeing process was an extension of what I had been doing on my Religion of One blog (blogger.relofone.com). I just blogged what I remembered seeing in strange dreams with no further analysis or judgment until I had documented the experiences as I remembered them. Alannah said it was important to free your imagination with the idea that anything is possible.

I could do this!

The day before my QHHT session, Alannah emailed me about how she worked. Part of her pre-session preparations involved contacting the client to remotely clear and align their chakras. I did not know what a chakra was. Alannah said she wanted me to come to the QHHT session already cleansed and ready to be hypnotized.

Chakra means wheel. It is a Sanskrit word. Each chakra center connects to the next chakra in line from your toes to your head.

I did not have to do anything to cleanse my chakras. The cleansing therapist remotely acted on my physical and spiritual bodies. She was going to contact my Higher Self through a medium.

Later in the evening (the night before my QHHT session),

I was emailed a digital recording of the remote clearing and chakra alignment session results.

Oh dear, I said to myself.

What I heard on the recording made absolutely no sense to me. I did not understand the meaning of the words used, the spirit names mentioned, or any of the processes of cleansing and chakra alignment used. I felt woefully unprepared for my journey into the spiritual realm the next day (11-01-2020) when I attended the QHHT session with Alannah.

On 05-11-2021, I took the time to listen to the pre-QHHT session remote clearing and chakra alignment recording more carefully and started to research the meaning of the pre-QHHT recording.

A voice in my head said,

Finally! I want to show you who I am!

…Who was talking to me in my head?

REVIEW OF MY PRE−QHHT CLEANSING RECORDING

Once I started to understand what was being said on the pre-QHHT cleansing and alignment session recording, I realized the pre-session recording statements were very important and insightful. There were two people on the pre-QHHT recording I listened to. Natasha Parvin facilitated the pre-QHHT cleansing and alignment session after Heather Stubbs had prepped herself and was ready to channel Dorothy (Heather's spirit guide). Heather went through a complicated process to get herself into a state where she could directly communicate with her spirit guide. Both Natasha and Heather have an amazing knowledge of the metaphysical realm. A lot was revealed to me on the recording from my remote, pre-QHHT cleansing/alignment session. My pre-QHHT and QHHT therapist's websites are as follows:

Natasha Parvin: www.soulstarenergetics.com and www.spiritanimalsart.com, https://www.youtube.com/channel/UC7lE6-xezKoku_5jgWorV-A

Heather Stubbs: https://quantumhealers.com/practitioner/heather-stubbs/

Alannah McKeehan: http://qhhtselfhealing.weebly.com

I needed to try to fully understand the amazing, spiritual insight these pre-QHHT session processes provided me so I could advance my soul to a higher level of consciousness in this lifetime. Heather was able to speak directly to my Higher Self through Dorothy. My Higher Self has lived many lives and has a detailed understanding of what I have done in the past, who I am now, and what my goals for the future are. Heather introduced me to someone in my soul family named Archangel Metatron. I knew then I had a lot of catching up to do so I could understand the significance of what Heather said in the recorded Pre-QHHT session.

Summary bullet points of important pre-QHHT recording statements follow…

- *Archangel Metatron is here. He is saying there is a soul connection– a soul family connection…*

- *My Higher Self: I am standing in my power. I am evolving. I am compassion.*

- *Contract in Egypt with dark forms to increase their energy.*

Reading the definitions of the seven different chakras provides you with a more holistic view of your wellness. Holistic medical clinics have become very popular in recent years. I know, from what I have read, that the origins of holistic medicine date back thousands of years to the time of the famous philosopher Pythagoras and even before Pythagoras.

Frankly, I initially thought this whole holistic healing idea was a bit of a sham.

It is not.

It was time for me to stop ignoring the whole metaphysical and holistic healing process. I needed to understand what I was being told by the well-known, reputable therapists I had the pleasure of working with. I first looked up the definitions of all the unknown words and concepts Heather mentioned in my recorded, remote pre-QHHT cleansing and alignment session …

Chakras allow the human body to balance and align the

different energy surrounding you to the point where you feel happy, healthy, and whole. Purging negative energy from your body, before a QHHT session, also opens up a person's energy level to pursue self-growth.

> *The seven main chakras are the most commonly accepted energy centers in all spiritual cultures that recognize the movement of energy through the human body. The chakras are gates to divine power and important tools for spiritual transformation, and as such, they have captivated and fascinated people for thousands of years.*[90]

The seven energy centers use the energy flowing into and around your body in different ways. Energy flows throughout the body through the seven chakras to perform different tasks in maintaining your body's functions, your spiritual awareness, and your overall feelings.

You can have too little or too much energy flowing into a particular chakra causing mental-related or other health-related issues. Negative, outside influences can have a long-lasting effect on your chakras and the flow of energy into, around, and out of your body.

---

90   The4. (n.d.). Chakra Points: 7 Chakra Locations In The Body. 7 Chakra Store. Retrieved December 26, 2022, from *https://7chakras-tore.com/blogs/news/chakra-points-locations*

Definitions of Chakras
Root Chakra

The root chakra, or Muladhara, is located at the base of your spine. It provides you with a base or foundation for life, and it helps you feel grounded and able to withstand challenges. Your root chakra is responsible for your sense of security and stability.

Sacral Chakra

The sacral chakra, or Svadhisthana, is located just below your belly button. This chakra is responsible for your sexual and creative energy. It's also linked to how you relate to your emotions as well as the emotions of others.

Solar plexus Chakra

The solar plexus chakra, or Manipura, is located in your stomach area. It's responsible for confidence and self-esteem, as well as helping you feel in control of your life.

Heart Chakra

The heart chakra, or Anahata, is located near your heart, in the center of your chest. It comes as no surprise that the heart chakra is all about our ability to love and show compassion.

Throat Chakra

The throat chakra, or Vishuddha, is located in your throat. This chakra has to do with our ability to communicate verbally.

Third eye Chakra

The third eye chakra, or Ajna, is located between your eyes. You can thank this chakra for a strong gut instinct. That's because the third eye is responsible for intuition. It's also linked to imagination.

Crown Chakra

The crown chakra, or Sahasrara, is located at the top of your head. Your Sahasrara represents your spiritual connection to yourself, others, and the universe. It also plays a role in your life's purpose.[91]

Definition of Holistic Medicine

Holistic…

Characterized by the belief that the parts of something are interconnected and can be explained only by reference to the whole:

The solution demands a holistic approach and a strategic

91   www.healthline.com/health/what-are-chakras#the-7-main-chakras.

vision of what can be achieved; poverty will need to be addressed holistically.

Medicine…

Characterized by the treatment of the whole person, taking into account mental and social factors, rather than just the symptoms of an illness:

Many people conclude that holistic medicines are beneficial. A truly alternative holistic medical practice. A holistic therapist.[92]

There have been formally trained doctors who have jumped ship and swam over to a more holistic community of healing. A holistic medical approach to living a healthier and happier life makes sense.

Have I run to a holistic healer?

No, I have not fully embraced the holistic approach yet. The holistic approach to medicine recognizes the fact a pill cannot cure everything, but the opposite is true as well. Holistic medicine cannot cure everything either. I was not going to try and heal my severe lower back pain using a form of holistic medicine (Reiki). It required extensive spinal fusion surgery to stop the lower spine from moving around.

What Is a Soul Family?

Soul Family — also known as Soul Group, Soul Pod, Soul

Cluster, or Star Family — consists of a group of souls who are part of a greater spiritual family who are connected in the Higher Dimensions and who reunite on Earth. Soul Families share the same soul purpose, a spiritual mission for learning, growth, and healing.

Essentially, your Soul Family shares the same oversoul, just like your biological family shares a common greater ancestry. On a soul level, each of the Soul Family members has their consciousnesses and also shares a unified collective consciousness.[93]

Your soul family is slightly different from your spirit guides and guardian angels as they are usually a collective group of beings to whom you are on similar frequency levels and energetically connected, related, and in tune. However, there are variations to this as occasionally a soul family member may be of angelic or seraphim origin, or if in physical form they may even be incarnated as your pet who watches over you.

Some of your soul family members travel with you and incarnate at the same time as you do, while others remain in higher frequency worlds. These relationships are often powerful and have a notion of emission that is shared by the various family members. Your soul family members who have incarnated here with you at the same time don't always have to be part of your bloodline family but can be

93   What Is Soul Family? | Aphrodite University | The Premier Divine Feminine University. (n.d.). Retrieved December 26, 2022, from https://aphroditeuniversity.org/soul-family/

anyone whom you strongly connect and resonate with and often share similar interests.

Connecting and working with your soul family may help protect and nurture them as they do their best to assist and support you.

Your soul family brings with them great wisdom that may not be previously fully accessible. This wisdom and knowledge may be able to assist you in remembering your life purpose and feeling like you have a mission in life. Your soul family's wisdom may be very useful in healing the wounds and assist in clearing things from your life that no longer serve you. Better life balance may also be established.

Your soul family may have worked spiritually on planet Earth in previous lifetimes and may be part of the collective of etheric elders, shamans, and protectors of planet Earth.[94]

My remote pre-QHHT session revealed that in the higher dimensions, I am directly related to Archangel Metatron. I share the same soul purpose — a spiritual mission for learning, growth, and healing.

I need to find out more about this relative. Metatron sounds like a name for a transformer in one of the Transformer movies.

---

94   Craig MacLennan, 'What Is A Soul Family?'' , (May 18, 2019). https://www.blissfullight.com/blogs/energy-healing-blog/what-is-a-soul-family

The Ancient Reason for My Asthma

I have asthma and I also have a super allergic reaction to sulfur in the air and from sulfites in food and wine. If my sulfur allergy came from ancient Egypt, my Higher Self must be very old in human years. I found the following Encyclopedia Britannica excerpt explaining the use of sulfur in prehistoric and ancient Egyptian times.

> *Prehistoric humans used sulfur as a pigment for cave painting; one of the first recorded instances of the art of medication is in the use of sulfur as a tonic. The combustion of sulfur had a role in Egyptian religious ceremonials as early as 4,000 years ago.*[95]

Reviewing the pre-QHHT remote recording, I noticed the remote therapist's spirit guide spoke directly to my Higher Self in my recording. Her spirit guide encouraged me to continue blogging in this life because it helps my eternal soul as well as those of others, to advance. Blogging can be an important tool to use for your spiritual advancement. In my opinion, remote cleansing and chakra alignment are also very valuable.

My go-to method of understanding what I am seeing is to research and recognize patterns of knowledge and behavior matching the strange stories and afterlife events I have experienced on my metaphysical journey. Other people have

95   *Sulfur | Definition, Element, Symbol, Uses, & Facts | Britannica.* (n.d.). Retrieved December 26, 2022, from https://www.britannica.com/science/sulfur

taken the time to research and publish articles/videos about the same spiritual experiences and objects I have seen in my visions and dreams. I have chosen reputable authors with extensive metaphysical knowledge to guide me along on my journey.

Chapter 6: My QHHT Session

INTRODUCTION

I followed a long driveway to Alannah's home. Old-growth trees lined the driveway and surrounded the house, giving it an aura of seclusion from the fast-paced world I had just driven from. In this serene setting, I could not help noticing a red, classic muscle car parked outside the house near one of these trees. The color red stuck in my mind for some reason.

Alannah answered the door. She was highly fit, and pretty.

Note: With the hot, red, muscle car parked in her driveway and Alannah's high-energy personality, I am thinking (seven and a half years later) that the QHHT session scene I experienced on 11/01/2020 is a classic déjà vu moment. My 11/24/2014–*Thank you, Angel with the Red Dress On!*

dream[96] (found in Appendix 1 of this book) matches the real vision of a hot, red muscle car in Alannah's driveway and resonates with Alannah's high-energy personality. Alannah helped guide me through some powerful QHHT visions, as you will find out in this chapter.

Alannah had us sit down at her dining room table to discuss what this session would be like. I felt relaxed and fully open to experiencing whatever my first QHHT session might bring. I told her I wanted to experience the full meal deal. She proceeded to enlighten me on valuable books I should read.

Then Alannah emphasized the fact that I needed to learn a way to protect myself during the QHHT session before I went into the actual session. I was not sure what I needed protection from, but I understood she had been on this journey with other people many times before. We agreed on a method of mental protection from negative energies I might be vulnerable to during my QHHT session.

Alannah also ran through a whole series of rituals to cleanse me before the hypnosis therapy began. She went through some cleansing rituals with crystals. Alannah recited cleansing passages I was required to repeat.

After the cleansing rituals, we went upstairs into one of several small bedrooms on the second floor. The interior of the house reminded me of a large ski lodge with bare pine wood

96   Major, M. 'Thank you Angel with the Red Dress On!', *Religion of One* (11-24-2014). https://relofone.blogspot. com/2014/11/11242014-thank-you-angel-with-red-dress.html

everywhere. I took off my shoes and crawled into a cozy bed, smothered with warm blankets and a comfy pillow. I closed my eyes as I lay on my back. Alannah started going through a prepared speech to get me to relax. The longer she spoke, the slower she talked. It brought me down to a very relaxed state. Her voice seemed to be quieter as she suggested I float out of my body onto a cloud to a place my spirit guide felt was important. Maybe to a previous life. She asked me to verbally explain what I was seeing without filtering anything out. I let go and just started to verbalize what I was seeing in my mind's eye. I felt I was in a state of relaxation beyond what I usually get to in a conscious state. I didn't feel hypnotized to the point I would start barking like a dog just because Alannah told me to. I checked the recordings afterward. She never once told me to bark like a dog...

TAPE 1

My initial visions were of steepled, medieval-looking buildings. I stood in a courtyard with soldiers guarding large, metal-clad doors. I was now a small child in pauper's clothing with a page haircut. As a four or five-year-old boy in this life, I looked up in awe at the armor-clad soldiers standing guard in the courtyard. All the metal armor the soldiers were wearing and the large metal-clad doors they were guarding, were embossed with ornate designs — almost like a complex, oriental embroidery. Each of the soldier's helmets had about an eight-inch dull, pewter-colored spike jutting out from the top of them.

The scene of my vision switched to a room where all the highly ornate metal was red and gold. There were also deep-red, velvet curtains and a shrine or throne embossed with ornate gold designs and trimmed with the same deep-red velvet as the curtains.

The throne room was empty.

My soul slowly drifted away from the medieval scene.

I passed a pristine, white, Mormon tabernacle-styled building with a big arched entryway and beautiful grounds.

My vision changed. I was floating above dark trees, following an exceptionally large white bird spirit (an owl or a hawk?) toward a strong white light within some fog. I felt comfortable following the bird spirit toward some bright, white clouds. I remember the bird was flying fast with extreme urgency and it took a lot of effort for me to keep up with it.

The bird spirit slowed down as we approached the white clouds. I saw a very tall figure dressed in a long, flowing white robe. He was holding a golden staff. I did not know if I was supposed to go any farther. I felt uncomfortable with this vision as I floated past the tall, imposing white-robed man. The tall figure in white reminded me of a shepherd of God. Was this an entrance into Heaven? Why was I here?

Suddenly, the white light turned to a hazy, blue light and shone on me from somewhere above in the fog. The large, white bird spirit I had been following disappeared from my vision. Floating forward through the blue fog, I came upon a vision of a *Mother Mary* figure cuddling a swaddled baby. My QHHT therapist asked me to look into Mary's eyes so she could communicate with me.

I said,

It was very nice...very serene...very cute. I don't know why I would see that.

The figure of Mary, the mother of Jesus, was looking down at the baby in her arms the whole time I saw her in my vision. I felt I did not have her attention, or she did not know I was floating by her.

Definition of Swaddling

Swaddling is an age-old practice of wrapping infants in blankets or similar cloths so that movement of the limbs is tightly restricted. Swaddling bands were often used to further restrict the infant. Swaddling fell out of favor in the 17th century.[97]

I continued past the scene of the swaddled baby and the Mother Mary figure. I noticed a very bright, white light in the distance and decided to float past Mother Mary to take a closer look at the source of the bright, white light.

So much energy but I don't know what it does.

Swaddling. (2022). In Wikipedia. https://en.wikipedia.org/w/index.php?title=Swaddling&oldid=1123937783

It took some effort to get to the bright, white light. I started noticing a bunch of pyramid-shaped, blue-colored crystals below me on a bed of white clouds.

Very strong, white light coming from the crystals. All very strange stuff.

My QHHT therapist asked me to describe the blue crystals and the surroundings so I could listen to my audio recording later and try to understand what they meant. I pointed out they were simple, triangular shapes. The color of the crystals was blue but more toward the turquoise blue side of the spectrum.

In the center of one crystal was a great white light...way up in the air like a beacon. I don't know where I'm at.

I laughed.

Alannah asked me,

Why did you laugh?

I said,

Because I probably shouldn't be here!

I laughed again in an almost defiant way. I have noticed the 'personality' of my soul, in dreams, is often a bit rebellious in attitude. In my dreams, I travel to places usually off-limits to other souls.

I further explained to Alannah that the blue, pyramid-shaped crystals were huge; and the white light was enormously powerful…

It is just energy going out into the cosmos and it's kind of cool. I think it's pretty powerful.

Alannah asks, *How does it affect you as you observe it?*

I said,

I am just confused. I don't know what it is.

Alannah encourages me,

You don't need to understand it. You just need to explain it.

I said,

It is just very powerful, and it jets out. I am going to try and jump in and see what happens!

Alannah asks for further details,

What happens when you do that?

I explain what is happening,

I don't know. I don't know. I'm just going. Like…I think I went someplace else.

I ended up floating above fields of green...

Rows of lush green. Rows of something growing. I don't know what it is.

I started getting distracted from my visions. I told Alannah my feet were getting cold.

Alannah said,

It's okay. It takes a lot... [of energy to follow your visions].

There was also an open window in the QHHT session room with kids playing outside. I found it very distracting. I have difficulty filtering other noises out. I am too easily distracted by the noise outside and my mind starts wandering to the children's conversation. Alannah covered my feet and closed the window in the session room to avoid the outdoor distractions. With her help, I was able to drift back into the superconscious state and observe another vision in a strange place.

After Alannah guided me back into a relaxed, superconscious state, she asked me to go to a place my spirit guide wanted me to see. I quickly entered a vision where I was standing at a podium with a long, silky graduation robe. I was in a stadium facing thousands of what I first interpreted as lost souls. The individual souls in the stadium were tall (seven feet or so), shriveled-up pieces of tree trunks. Alannah asked what I was saying to the graduation audience.

119

All I said was, *I love you all.*

I was trying to interpret to the QHHT therapist what I was seeing as the vision occurred. It was difficult for me to understand this vision in real-time. Why was I envisioning this?

I relayed what I was seeing to Alannah,

These lost souls are just waiting and looking for direction from me.

Alannah asked me what I was saying to the lost souls. I told her I was simply having them come to me on stage and I would hug them. An extraordinarily strong beam of white light shone on my back the whole time I was on the podium. By hugging the lost souls, I was able to transfer a portion of this white light to each of the souls I hugged.

At first, I was sure these souls were the worst of the worst bunch, and this was their last-ditch effort to be saved from all their warped and evil ways. The more I interacted with these lost souls, the more confused I became. You would think the worst of the worst bunch of lost souls would emanate guilt, pain, and even hate. All I felt coming from them was total silence and an amazing degree of patience for such a large audience. These souls did not speak. They just waited patiently to be directed or graduated to a higher plane of existence.

Later, as I left the QHHT therapist's house, she told me she often hugs this huge, probably hundred-year-old tree next to her entryway. Her whole property, where she lives, is covered in large evergreen trees. Alannah proceeded to hug the closest large tree. I followed suit and hugged the tree as well. I wrapped my arms around the tree and gave it a couple of knocks using my knuckles. I noticed a uniquely pitched sound of hardwood as I gave the tree a couple of raps.

I said,

I wonder if each tree has its own unique sound.

I told Alannah about an article I had read in a science magazine explaining how large, old trees often reduced the amount of water they sucked up from the ground if a baby tree was within its massive root system. The article said this selfless act of the large, old trees to nurture their baby trees nearby was a sign of a complex, sentient entity… Trees displayed a feeling of compassion toward the baby tree.

Alannah then gave me a sweet hug with our COVID-19 masks securely attached to our faces and I went home. I was tired after the visions and intense energy I had experienced.

Remembering the vision of going past a tall shepherd dressed in a long, white robe and seeing the vision of Mother Mary, I realized the image of Mother Mary nurturing the baby in her arms exactly matches the nurturing of baby trees by older trees around it. The concept of nurturing and compassion in a blue aura of light is an important concept to take away and mull over from this QHHT session.

Definition of Compassion

Sympathetic pity and concern for the sufferings or misfortunes of others.

E.g. 'The victims should be treated with compassion'

Definition of Nurture

Care for and encourage the growth or development of.

E.g. 'Jarrett was nurtured by his parents in a close-knit family'

Help or encourage the development of.

E.g. 'My father nurtured my love of art'

Cherish (a hope, belief, or ambition).

E.g. 'For a long time, she had nurtured the dream of buying a shop.'

I sent the following email to Alannah on 11-05-2020.

I think I figured out a better explanation of the vision I had in your session where I was dressed in a graduation robe passing on the white light I was channeling into the six or seven-foot, shriveled-up brown things. What puzzled me about my vision is I felt no emotions coming from the thousands of shriveled, brown entities I saw in the stadium. They were just waiting. You would think that if they were extremely tormented souls trying to find their way, they *would be filled with all sorts of guilt and negativity.*

After mulling it over and remembering the first thing you did when we walked out of your house was the fact you had a great desire to show me how you like to hug a tree at the end of a session. Then, you hugged me. I finally connected this real-life event to my vision of shriveled, brown souls. Connecting real events to visions and dreams is what I have been trying to perfect and understand for the past fifteen years.

Most likely I was graduating tree souls to another level of consciousness by hugging each one and transferring to each tree soul in the stadium the white light to elevate their souls to the next level. It just makes sense the souls of a mature tree would still be very tall.

Maybe my hugs are a transfer of positive energy to souls ready to graduate to the next level. Tell me if you feel more enlightened now.

I like this new path of enlightenment I'm on. Pretty Cool!

TAPE 2

I cannot remember if I stopped the session to take a restroom break or if Alannah had to switch to a new Tape 2 audio file. It took a lot of concentrated effort and energy to keep pushing myself further into the unknown via these visions. I had to willfully look around in my visions and verbally communicate, without judgment or hesitation, what I was seeing. I was not understanding a lot of these visions at the time they occurred. The visions seemed to cross the boundaries of Time and Space and tap into thousands of years of history and knowledge I was not previously aware of at the time of my QHHT session. I was determined to take this guided journey with Alannah. Afterward, she told me she had personally not experienced what I had seen in my visions. She said there were a few others she had helped guide into a superconscious state of mind who did have similar experiences to mine.

The journey continued…

Alannah asked, *What are you aware of?*

I said,

It's dark.

Tell me about the darkness, Alannah said.

I proceeded to describe the scene I was floating through in my mind. Instead of the sky being above me, my vision showed the sky was to the right of me. Pure darkness was in front of me. I felt like I was in between worlds.

Alannah encouraged me to just drift and float for a moment to get my bearings straight. Then I would know which way to go.

How strange this vision was, clouds floating, perpendicular, on my right side and pure darkness in front of me. This scene was about to get even stranger.

I am going inside the pupil of a big...eye!

I was feeling a little uncertain if this was a good idea,

I don't know...

Alannah encouraged me with her soft, reassuring voice,

So go inside the big eye. Be curious and explore...Moving inside the big eye. So, what does it feel like to be inside a big eye?

I said,

It is very weird. Weird. I think this is a weird world. It's all...Looks like a bunch of folded, paper buildings...

These folded, paper buildings were to the left of my line of sight.

In front of me, it was, *Dark, dark, dark. Everything is dark.*

The folded buildings to my left were made up of various rectangular shapes and were colored a light grey.

It was like Japanese paper art or something. I laugh.

Alannah wanted me to keep moving my vision around the

buildings and look at different perspectives to see if I could make out any interesting details other than the fact they just looked like a group of light grey Japanese origami-shaped buildings in deep, dark space. I was getting bored with the scene because it was so generic. Alannah tried to encourage me to explore the buildings more, but I felt my bodiless soul start to drift away until Alannah asked me to take a harder look.

She said, *Amazing! Do you see any energies?*

My viewpoint of the origami buildings changed to a slightly elevated view of this strange structure floating in space.

I said, *Yes. All underneath them* [the group of origami buildings floating in space] ...*It is all magnetic energy. It's just very weird. I don't know why I am there.*

Alannah reassured me,

I'll figure that out for you. Your only job is to be curious and flow along.

I trusted Alannah. She had plenty of previous experience safely placing several other clients in an enhanced state of consciousness using her certified QHHT techniques.

Okay, I say that now—over a year after I had the QHHT session but...The next set of visions I had during my very first QHHT session started to freak me out...a lot!

I said in surprise,

Oh! I think something...There are roots!

She had taught me some protection techniques to ward off negative energy before I entered my hypnotic state. She said I needed some tools to protect myself on my journey into my mind's eye. I envisioned a silver enclosure. It was a protective shell of translucent, silver material that I felt protected me from any negative energy that might try to attack me. I think this translucent shell was in the shape of a pyramid. It came in handy during the QHHT session. I was so inexperienced on this journey in my mind.

I said,

I don't think this is a good place. I have to protect myself
and go back into the silver thing.

Alannah encouraged me,

Okay. Go back in the silver thing. Nothing can harm you.
Observe what is going on.

I nervously responded,

Those roots were trying to get in me!

Alannah pressed for more details about the roots. I told her they came from underneath the building structure, floating in dark space, where the magnetic energy waves came from.

The vision of a large, hairy, fleshy-looking root with patches of sparse, dark stubbled hair on it, was poking at my belly button. I felt like I was being violated and I started to panic a little. I am not one to back away in fear. I usually get mad. This vision had me running back to the safety of my silver pyramid. Thinking back on it now, the root looked like the head of the character from the *Sponge Bob* cartoon series *Patrick Star* except, in my vision, the fleshy root had no eyes and had thick, sparse black stubble all over its body.

I said, *It was just gross. Blackness; roots.*

Alannah asked,

Are you protected now? ... Do you have a body?

I replied,

Yeah, I have a body. I am a little white boy. White.

I could not sense any distinguishing features of my body. I just felt it was a normal body of a small boy with no distinguishable features. I was bathed in pure white light.

My vision continued.

I am standing in this ... bathed in white. I am just standing there being protected. I'm scared to go anywhere, now. I don't know what to do.

128

Alannah repeated what I said a lot during the QHHT session so she clearly understood the image I was seeing. She truly believed whatever I was envisioning had a special spiritual meaning. It was being communicated to me by my spirit guides or my Higher Self. These visions were important and enlightening to me, even though I did not understand their real meaning at the time. That is why the sessions are digitally recorded and given to you to listen to later. What at first seemed to be bizarre and silly visions turned out to have powerful meanings and messages.

Okay. You are a scared white boy in white light.

I replied,

I don't know. It is just a cocoon in there, and I am just protecting myself like crazy.

Alannah must have heard some pretty bizarre descriptions of visions from other clients while under hypnosis. My situation in deep space did not seem to alarm her at all...yet.

Alannah stated,

Well, your physical body now is fine, so let's see what happens. They [my spirit guides] are showing you a significant event. You need a guide. You can call for a guide and they'll come and be with you.

I requested a spirit guide...

I want to see a guide to help me. Oh…There's a nice light area. There you go!

Alannah asked me, *What do they look like?*

I said,

They are just white blobs.

I described them as *just white blobs* because they were currently, in deep space, coming toward me from far away. As the white blobs came closer to me, I noticed they had little white dots in the middle of their nondescript bodies.

They are surrounding me. I am surrounded by my white blobs. I am very peaceful now. I am a white dot in the middle now and they are surrounding me…

Alannah asked me to watch the scene as an observer to try and understand why they sent me to the origami buildings floating in deep space.

I was not too keen on revisiting the origami structures with the hairy, fleshy root popping out of the bottom of them in deep, dark space.

It's scary. It was…attaching to me. Very, very alien, but I got out of there.

Alannah wanted to know if I was still the small boy in the cocoon.

There was a lot of activity starting to surround me as I floated in my protective cocoon in deep space...

Okay, so I'm starting to see a lot of alien beings now, but...

Alannah was showing some signs of alarm,

Alien beings? ... Okay. So, what do the alien beings look like?

I replied, *Really big heads and very skinny bodies and ... They don't pay much attention to me as much as...I just see them floating by. They were almost like spirits.*

It was taking a lot of energy for me to focus on this intense scene but I started to become bored with it after a while because nothing more was happening. Everything I described was just floating aimlessly in limbo around me in my protective cocoon.

I want to go to someplace fun and interesting. This is boring.

The real truth is I did not understand any of the bizarre, deep space scenes I was describing under hypnosis at that moment.

Alannah encouraged me to stick around and float in deep space for a while.

But it's okay. They will show you what's important. It's important. They'll show you what's important.

I acquiesced, *Okay.*

Alannah asked to explain the details of the scene I was now in.

Does it feel like you have a body?

I said,

I have someone next to me. I have a body.

Alannah asked,

What does he look like?

It's just a big, round, raincoat type, poncho deal…and some people around me are being nice and they are supporting me., I said.

Alannah asked,

Are the alien heads still floating around you?

Yeah., I acknowledged,

They are transparent.

Alannah was suddenly more alarmed. She asked, in a strained, even tone,

They are transparent?

I said, *Their heads are transparent, yeah!*

The Tape 2 recording session was paused at this point and Alannah read from a canned script in what I think was a QHHT training manual. She was concerned for my safety and started a process of purging the strange, alien beings surrounding me in my vision in deep space.

Although the vision was alarming to me during my actual QHHT session, I look back at it now and both the white blobs and aliens surrounding me were not threatening me in the vision. The white blobs were very nice to me. There was even someone who materialized right next to me in my protective cocoon. I did not seem alarmed at this vision until I saw the transparent-headed aliens.

There is a lot written about a very common process of people who have already died coming to greet a person's soul immediately after they die. Many people have come back from a dead state, for one reason or another. Some say they were greeted by relatives in their dead state. Michael Newton has proposed the people greeting you are there to help you transition to the afterlife. They are a part of the group you were in before reincarnating to Earth and have a common soul family connection with you in the afterlife. Michael Newton's proposal is the same as what my pre-QHHT alignment and cleansing therapist told me about my soul family connection to Archangel Metatron.

I described myself as a white boy floating alone in a deep, dark space during my scary Tape 2, QHHT session vision. This reminds me of a previous passage from David Rippy's book,

The Immortal Soul; the Journey to Enlightenment.[98]

In the conclusions section of Chapter 3 of this book, I quoted David Rippy's statement,

All souls have a 'color', starting at white…. Similar to a spectrum or chakras, a soul advances through various stages in their soul evolution, earning advancing colors as they evolve. After eons, souls eventually attain the purple color designation, meaning they're highly evolved.[99]

The image of me as a small, white boy floating in a deep, dark space represented a new soul passing on to the afterlife for the very first time. The figure with the transparent head matches Chapter Four of The Reluctant Messenger Returns titled *Life Force Weavers*. Candice Sanderson describes life force weavers as transparent figures…

The figure was unlike any human body I had seen. The skin was completely transparent and, within its frame, floated different-sized translucent bubbles.[100]

As a part of transitioning into the afterlife, each person's life force weaver exits from their body.

---

98   Rippy, David. The Immortal Soul; the Journey to Enlightenment: Case Studies of Hypnotically Regressed Subjects and their Afterlives. David Rippy. Kindle Edition

99   Rippy, D., p. 218.

100   Sanderson, Candice M. The Reluctant Messenger Returns: An Unexpected Adventure into the Angelic Realm (p. 49). Clark Press. Kindle Edition.

Life Force Weavers are the adhesive that keeps the memory orbs together. Their presence defines life… Life Force Weavers unravel and retreat from the physical body upon death …[101]

Candice Sanderson's vision of transparent figures was just as strange as my QHHT vision of the transparent-headed figure in deep space. I did not know this transparent figure in my QHHT session vision had just been released from the young, white soul's Earthly body as it transitioned into the afterlife for the very first time until I read The Reluctant Messenger Returns: An Unexpected Adventure into the Angelic Realm. It is comforting to know someone else has had the same bizarre vision I had. It relates exactly to the same thing my vision was trying to explain to me. This was part of the process for transitioning to the afterlife after passing away.

I have documented a few dreams where I am being asked by a voice in my head or in the background of my dream scene to interact with specific souls I can see in the dream and help them pass on to the afterlife. I am asked to encourage them to move to the light and enter the afterlife without any fear or remorse.[102]

My QHHT visions became stranger and even more unbelievable to me as I continued my session with Alannah.

---

101   Sanderson, Candice, The Reluctant Messenger Returns: An Unexpected Adventure into the Angelic Realm (pp. 52,53). Clark Press. Kindle Edition.
102   Major, M. 'Helping a Lost Soul to Heaven', *Religion of One* (10-29-2016). https://relofone.blogspot.com/2016/10/10-29-2016-helping-lost-soul-to-heaven.html

Jumping into the vast sea of metaphysical knowledge and energy under hypnosis could have been dangerous to my mind and my body without Alannah's guidance. I had no idea what I was doing and what would happen when I signed up for a QHHT session.

The pre-QHHT session exercises, which I did at home, taught me to keep my mind open to any vision I could see. I was in a relaxed state and floated along in my mind beyond space and time to places my spirit guides wanted me to see. The visions slowly became visible to me as I gently allowed my mind to float forward. I believe I pictured my mind floating forward on a soft, white, billowy cloud.

The visions I witnessed during the QHHT session were very foreign to me. The soft, hazy auras of light I saw at the very beginning of the session became incredibly powerful beams of intense white light in later visions. My body was in a relaxed state, yet my mind was functioning at a very high energy state with heightened awareness. I was able to explain to Alannah what I was seeing but was not at all able to clearly understand what these strange visions meant. I kept saying things like,

I don't know why I am here.

It took proactive energy on my part to follow the visions. If I had just laid back and not pursued a particular scene currently in my mind, I believe the scene would have slowly faded away. I would then have continued to float along into what seemed like deep, starless space until I noticed some other strange scene

I was passing by. If I found myself drifting past a strange vision, or floating in what appeared to be deep, dark space, I had to consciously decide to stop drifting and jump into the scene to get a closer look. Alannah was good at prompting me to,

Take a closer look.

Alannah had successfully purged my mind of negative thoughts, entities, and energies after my intense encounter with the transparent alien vision in deep, outer space.

I continued my journey under mild hypnosis and immediately drifted into another vision. This was a place of rest. There were two other reasons I felt comfortable continuing with the session after initially being frightened. I felt I was able to successfully protect myself when I entered threatening scenes in my mind, using the method Alannah and I had agreed upon before we began. Alannah also kept emphasizing I was in these visions as an observer. I simply needed to report what I saw without fear. I did not need to try and understand what I was seeing.

TAPE 2 CONTINUED...

A Place of Rest

My QHHT session visions became even more intense. After a while, I started seeing extremely powerful, blinding beams of white light, mind-bending visions of spiritual beings, angels in all their glory, and historical scenes covering hundreds of years of human history. The scope and intensity of the visions I had during a single QHHT session were way beyond my normal, nightly dreams; I was truly in a superconscious state of mind.

Continuing with my QHHT session experience, I said to Alannah,

I think this is where I live in my afterlife and it's nice...
Nice place, I am just going home. I get to rest.

Alannah presses me to look around and explain my surroundings.

There are warm, yellow lights as I approach my place.
It looks like I have a townhouse. I'm on the top floor or something.

This is a nice, quiet place, there's nobody... Nobody around but...

It's a big place, so I know there are people around. It's just my place; there is no one.

This is where I go to rest...

It's nice and warm there.

It's almost an orangey-pink color. Something you would see in Spain. It is Spanish...

I just feel safe there. It's a place of peace.

That's where I go...

I see an angel.

Alannah asks me,

What does the angel look like?

I reply,

It's just there. Observing me. It's just making sure I'm happy.

That's nice.

It has wings.

Alannah replies,

Wings. Is it male or female?

I tell her it is,

Female. Just coming over to check up on me.

Alannah again prompts me to try and learn more. I think she senses I am getting too comfortable just resting.

Alannah says,

Does the angel want to take you anywhere else or show you anything? Maybe a part of you can stay there, but the angel can talk through you to me or show you other things that are important in this lifetime… While watching, you, meanwhile, can rejuvenate your physical, spiritual, mental, and emotional bodies in this place of rest. What does the angel suggest?

My voice on the tape first says *nine* (Or am I saying *no* in German?). I am afraid of extreme heights in my mortal life and apparently under hypnosis, as well ...

I explain,

They are suggesting I go and look at the nice blue sky above me, but...I don't know.

We are pretty high up, I don't know. There's not much above me. Maybe another little terrace.

And I am just looking at a nice, peaceful sky. It's nice. It's a place of rest. There are no worries. Just rest. I think this is what she wanted to show me.

It's not dark and black like that other place. It was blue and serene. And a beautiful sky. It was nice. The other place was yucky.

Alannah has been formally trained in Reiki healing. I was not at all familiar with Reiki before going into the QHHT session.

What is Reiki?

Reiki is a Japanese technique for stress reduction and relaxation that also promotes healing. It is administered by

140

'laying on hands' and is based on the idea that an unseen 'life force energy' flows through us and is what causes us to be alive. If one's 'life force energy' is low, then we are more likely to get sick or feel stressed, and if it is high, we are more capable of being happy and healthy.

The word Reiki is made of two Japanese words. 'Rei' means 'God's Wisdom or the Higher Power'...'Ki' ... is 'life force energy'. So, Reiki is actually 'spiritually guided life force energy'.[103]

Chi is the traditional Chinese equivalent to the life force energy word *Ki*. Chi is important in traditional Chinese philosophy, religion, and medicine.[104]

Alannah told me, after the QHHT session, all the lights dimmed in the bedroom and a subdued, blue glow filled the room when I was explaining to her my vision of the angel.

She knew my vision of the angel was real when she witnessed the dimming blue room right in front of her eyes. The angel was hovering slightly above me and behind me where I was sitting in my townhouse of rest. The angel was very tall, slender, and had a huge wing span. She was bathed in blue light.

My *restful place* vision continued.

---

103   Administrator, R. (2014, October 15). *What is Reiki?* https://www.reiki.org/faqs/what-reiki

104   *What is Chi? - Definition from Yogapedia. (n.d.).* Yogapedia. Com. Retrieved December 26, 2022, from http://www.yogapedia.com/definition/10360/chi

And I feel good; fresh air; almost like a fresh breeze. Fresh breeze, wonderful.

Very nice clean air. Clean air. My lungs are clearing up.

I think so. Real good.

Alannah follows this train of thought. She begins to guide me into a whole-body Reiki healing process. She starts by asking me:

Excellent. Do they need to do anything else to help you with asthma? What was causing asthma

I replied,

Anything dark. Dark, dark. Dark. Dark things.

Alannah asks,

So where did it originate? This life or another life?

I reply,

Another world. Another dimension.

Remember I am not on Earth, in my mind, as I tell her where I think asthma came from. The implication is I 'caught' asthma, recently, on Earth in this particular lifetime.

A common theory of souls reincarnated on Earth is they are

coming back to Earth to learn specific lessons to advance their eternal souls further along the path toward God.

Alannah prompts me further,

When was the very first time this soul experienced asthma?

I reply,

It's... recently.

I responded with the first idea to come to my mind, without judgment, as they taught me to do in the mind-opening lessons Alannah had sent me to practice at home ahead of time.

Alannah asks,

So, what are you going to put where asthma used to be in the lungs?

I respond,

Light.

Alannah asks,

So, what was the purpose of Marcas experiencing asthma in this lifetime?

I am hesitant and finally reply,

Not sure... If I don't feel pain, I wouldn't know the difference.

Alannah responds,

But now he experienced that and he can release it completely. Is that correct?

And they're putting white light there for you now, as you're in the resting place.

I explain to Alannah what I am feeling,

It is a lot easier to breathe.

Alannah speaks to the healing angels directly,

Is that all Marcas needed to know about healing asthma?

I further explain,

You have to experience pain to see the light.

My pre-QHHT cleansing therapist channeled another reason for my problems with asthma from my Higher Self ...

Asthma is a preordained condition to teach me the importance and Earthly gift of breathing.

The Reiki healing process was applied to my right shoulder, my lower back, my two teeth scheduled to be pulled out very soon, all of the skin on my body, and my head.

My body had started absorbing the roots of two of my perfectly healthy molars for some rare and unknown reason. This dental condition is called root resorption.[105]

My body was also absorbing all of the colored pigment in my skin. I had a disease called Vitiligo.

As a side note, here it is two years after my QHHT session and I have noticed my Vitiligo has been put into remission. I am gaining pigment back in my skin now. The scientific reason for the remission of my Vitiligo is I had to quit drinking and go on a small dosage of a very powerful chemotherapy drug called Methotrexate for another problem I had with pain from swelling joints. Methotrexate dampens my immune system response. My body's immune system is no longer overreacting and absorbing the pigments in my skin. I am now open to the non-scientific idea that the healing angels' energy, which began two years earlier, has also been a part of my amazing recovery from Vitiligo.

The Reiki healing process permanently healed the pain in my upper right arm. I broke my upper, right arm when I fell off a ladder. Bolts were used to fasten a long rod pushed through the bone marrow of my right humerus to hold it in one piece while the bone healed around it. The pain was caused by loosened bolts rubbing against my upper arm tendons. I felt my upper right arm was where the angels spent the most time trying to heal my body. I could see a white, healing light course to the

105   *Root Resorption – An Unusual Phenomenon.* (n.d.). Retrieved December 26, 2022, from https://www.deardoctor.com/inside-the-magazine/issue-28/root-resorption/.

places in my body they were healing.

The angels hinted they did not get rid of all of my asthma. When Alannah specifically asked whether they got rid of my asthma, I told her they got rid of most of it. The same response was given when they tried to heal my lower back. I still have asthma but it is well controlled with asthma medicine now. I flew down to the Mayo Clinic in Phoenix, Arizona for extensive lower back surgery to permanently fix in place the last two vertebrae in my back to my tailbone. I was not ready to trust my extremely delicate and painful lower back to be fully healed with Reiki. My two lower vertebrae had popped out of the spinal cord support structure. The loose vertebrae would randomly move around and poke my central nerve channel.

The pain was so unpredictable and so excruciating I opted to take the traditional, proven way to heal my lower back pain. I had been living with this pain for several years and it just seemed to be getting worse. I also had my two traumatized teeth pulled out. I was shocked by the fact my body had chosen to slowly terminate two perfectly good teeth in my body. I am in the long process of getting teeth implants to replace the missing teeth. The endodontist I saw was not sure why my body decided to absorb the roots of two of my teeth. I felt extremely uneasy taking the leap of faith to rely solely on Reiki to fix a very serious, unknown problem close to my brain.

Alannah had the angels scan my whole body and look for issues they might be able to heal. I find it fascinating that during my Reiki healing process, my healing angels identified an anomaly in my neck causing a bottleneck in the energy flow to my head. Months later, I found out I had a pseudo aneurysm (a bulging wall of the carotid artery on the left side of my neck). The neurosurgeon I saw identified this condition and immediately prescribed 325mg of aspirin a day for the rest of my life so there was less of a chance of blood being caught in this bulge. The formation of a blood clot in the bulge of the carotid artery could loosen and go to my brain. A blood clot entering the brain could cause a stroke.

I admit, I have many health problems but I do not dwell on them. I choose to focus on the positive aspects of each day of my life. I am one of those people who just live day to day. I am easily overwhelmed when I have too many things to think of at once, and my brain simply shuts down the whole thought process, so I am only able to concentrate on one thing at a time.

Alannah flushed out other revelations during the lengthy Reiki healing portion of the QHHT session. It is amazing to me how my Higher Self and healing angels were responding directly to Alannah's questions. This was like the pre-QHHT therapist's conversation with my Higher Self.

Some of my body's health issues are directly related to my past experiences in this life and previous lives on Earth. I found out it is called karmic baggage.[106] My Vitiligo is a soul contract. It is a non-physical agreement I made between my Higher Self and

---

106   *Ways To Get Rid Of Karmic Baggage*. (n.d.). Retrieved December 26, 2022, from https://www.speakingtree.in/article/ways-to-get-rid-of-karmic-baggage

my soul family before I was reincarnated.[107]

I will summarize what the healing angels revealed to me in my QHHT session about my Vitiligo. Contracts are agreed upon as lessons to be learned in this specific reincarnation on Earth.

Alannah asks, *So what was causing the Vitiligo? The discoloration of your skin, could they work on that for you?*

I respond,

It's not important.

Alannah further prompts me, *They said it's not important?*

I say, *Yeah, it's not important.*

Alannah repeats, *Not important.*

I clarify further, *… That maybe pigments are not important. That's a lesson to be learned. Right? That's a lesson.*

Alannah asks for further clarification, *What kind of lesson is it that skin color is not important?*

I again respond with confidence, *It's not important.*

Alannah asks, *And why is it not important?*

My eternal soul responds…

Because everyone's the same. Because everyone is the same and the exterior appearance of skin color doesn't matter.

---

107   Boomer, S. (2020, February 9). *What are Soul Contracts and How Do They Work? - Awake and Align.* https://awakeandalign.com/soul-contracts/

I responded to Alannah with more confidence than I would normally respond to her if I were fully awake. When fully awake, I did not have a lot of confidence in expressing my opinions about the root cause of my health problems, let alone any other metaphysical reasons for my current behavior or existence on Earth. I was there to listen and learn. I was not expecting to even talk to her, in any depth, about the history behind all my health problems. I believe my Higher Self was speaking directly to Alannah during a lot of the Reiki portion of my QHHT session.

Michael Newton, in Journey of Souls, also identifies this idea of contracts of learning agreed upon by one's Higher Self and one's spirit guides before being reincarnated on Earth.

Dr. N: You sound a little depressed at the prospect of an intimate conversation with your guide about your last life.

S: (defensively) Because I blew it! I have to see him explain why things didn't work out. Life is so hard! I try to do it right ... but ...

Dr. N: Do what right?

S: (with anguish) I had an agreement with Clodees to work on setting goals and then following through. He had expectations for me as Ross. Damn! Now I have to face him with this ...

Dr. N: You don't feel you met the contract you had with your advisor about lessons to be learned as Ross?

S: (impatiently) No, I was terrible. And, of course, I'll have to do it all over again. We never seem to get it perfect. (pause) You know, if it weren't for Earth's beauty ... the birds ... flowers ... trees ... I would never go back. It's too much trouble.

Dr. N: I can see you are upset, but don't you think ...

S: (breaks in with agitation) You can't get away with a thing, either. Everybody here knows you so well. There is nothing I can keep from Clodees.[108]

It was important for me to find other documented cases matching my QHHT visions and recorded conversations. This is the ultimate verification of my pretty bizarre experiences. I was beyond my conscious mind's eye. I was seeing a far greater view of reality through my superconscious mind's eye.

I am truly in awe of the knowledge and wisdom of my eternal soul (i.e. my Higher Self). Through my superconscious mind, I can view pieces of my past lives and absorb portions of the total wisdom and knowledge available to me when I am in a heightened state of mind. If my pre-QHHT cleansing therapist is correct, I was given access to visions from my ancient soul family, including Archangel Metatron himself.

It is wonderful a gift to have an increased awareness of the subtle and not-so-subtle messages from my spirit guides at just the right time to help me write this book and find answers to the questions I have.

For example, I am often immediately drawn to a specific

108   Newton, *Journey of Souls*, pp. 58-59.

video title when randomly browsing *YouTube.com* and *Amazon Prime*. I get a strong feeling I need to watch a particular video right away. The timely and relevant information revealed to me in these videos often serves to enhance the recent knowledge I have gained on a subject. I believe I am encouraged to review certain videos at specific times by spiritual guidance.

Cari Palmer just happened to release two videos featuring a discussion with a very enlightened person who has created a therapy method to help you develop and understand where your eternal soul is currently at on its path toward evolving your cosmic conscience to a higher level of spiritual enlightenment.[109]

The QHHT session visions I reviewed in this book were way beyond my metaphysical knowledge and wisdom at the time I went into the session. I especially needed help interpreting the next portion of my QHHT session because the visions get even further away from my naïve notions of the afterlife and any previous dreams of the afterlife I have experienced. I expected to see and have meaningful conversations with some of my deceased relatives. I did not see any deceased relative that I recognized.

After listening to just a few minutes of the first YouTube video Cari Palmer created with Maria Elana Mexia, I am now able to easily recognize the four modules Maria Elana defines in her Evolutionary Process of healing and enlightenment.

I believe it will also help the reader of this book to identify

109 'Interview with Cari Palmer by Maria Elena,' *Evolutionary Learning, Conscious Evolution and Therapies*, mariaelenamexia.com, (4 Jan, 2022).

and categorize what module I was working on during specific QHTT session visions.[110]

The Four Modules of Healing by Maria Elena Mexia

I just finished discussing the Reiki Healing portion of my Tape 2 QHHT session recordings when writing my book. Then, on a multiple eleven date (02-25-2022), I discovered Cari Palmer's latest YouTube video interviews with Maria Elena. I have had email correspondence with Cari Palmer because she and Candice Sanderson created a whole series of YouTube videos I watched when I needed them the most. I trust Cari's judgment and sources of information. Cari had taken some Monroe Institute courses with Maria Elena.

Maria Elena's Four Modules of Healing offers you a way to understand who you are. She identifies certain frequencies she defines just for you to use to get the best version of who you need to be in this life. It is a method that allows you to fulfill the soul contract(s) or the mission your Higher Self established before your current soul was reincarnated on Earth. I ended up having specific QHHT session visions in every one of Maria Elena's four modules without even knowing it. The amount of pure white energy flowing through the visions of my body during my QHHT session was extraordinary. I wanted to understand how this could happen and what it meant.

Maria Elena's process for conscious enlightenment is called

110   Michael Press (Director). (2015, April 14). *Your Mission, Should You Choose To Accept It....* https://www.youtube.com/watch?v=0TiqXFssKMY

the 'Evolutionary Process'. She can create a simple map of your soul. Cari Palmer said she had done this with Maria Elena and it was very enlightening. It is created separately for each client and shows each client where their eternal soul is currently at in their Evolutionary Process toward a higher frequency of spiritual enlightenment.

In the first training module, you work on traumatic issues in this life's past and set yourself free from carrying the weight of those negative experiences forward on your journey to a higher level.

Maria Elena states,

You are not your past.

She says you must identify your self-defeating past behaviors to move forward with what matters to you physically, mentally, and spiritually in this life. If you take the time to learn why you are currently acting a certain way and you realize it was something in your past, then know you can drop those past burdensome barriers to achieve the best version of your whole self in this lifetime ... spiritually, mentally, and physically. This is what Alannah was trying to help me understand in the Reiki healing portion of my session. Alannah asked my Higher Self why certain soul contracts I had were important to accomplish in my lifetime.

The second training module looks into your past lives here on Earth. I am talking about the previous incarnations you have lived on Earth or elsewhere in the universe.

The idea of reincarnation matches many of my most baffling dreams about my afterlife. In my afterlife dreams, I am often very rebellious, but not hateful. This conclusion is based on the dreams I listed in *Appendix 1*.

I blame it on my ADD.[111]

My previous dreams have revealed my spirit guides have been frustrated with my past behavior. They have not trusted me to follow the rules in the afterlife and during reincarnations. (Ref. Appendix 1).

In my current life, I am on a fairly high dosage of an ADD medicine designed to enhance my ability to concentrate on one task and see it through to completion. I still jumped into the QHHT session without being very well-prepared, so my medicine is not foolproof.

If you read the twenty-nine real-life client cases Michael Newton discusses in his book[112] or the case studies in David Rippy's The Immortal Soul: The Journey To Enlightenment, it becomes obvious that others, like me, have not always accomplished the goals (contracts) they agreed to work on during their previous incarnations. It has become clear to me that afterlife living is very structured and there are specific lessons each eternal soul must work on to advance toward a divine level of spiritual enlightenment.

---

111   Red Bull Records (Director). (2014, April 21). *AWOLNATION - Sail (Official Music Video)*. https://www.youtube.com/watch?v=t-gIqecROs5M

112   Michael Newton, *Journey of Souls*, Llewellyn Worldwide, Kindle Edition.

Alannah asked questions to understand why I had certain health problems in my current life and whether I could now heal myself. She was directly asking my Higher Self and the angels, who were healing my body with powerful beams of white light and other powerful beams from different colored crystals. She asked them what lessons I was supposed to learn in this lifetime.

An example of lessons learned in this lifetime for me is...

The color of your skin is not important. We are all the same at a spiritual level of existence.

Maria Elena's approach is the same as Alannah's. To achieve the best version of yourself, in this lifetime, you have to tune into and work with specific healing frequencies. My QHHT vision was of angels using different colored crystals to heal my body.

Maria Elena explains her healing method must also get to the point of healing by searching for and releasing some of the mental and physical issues you inherited from your current life and your past lives. If you can identify, acknowledge, and let go of some of the burdensome experiences from your current past and previous lives, you will feel much lighter as you progress toward Maria Elena's third module. You will then begin to learn more about your true being ... your light being.

The following QHHT conversations exactly match Maria Elena's comments. The conversation between my Higher Self and my QHHT therapist, Alannah, was truly a beautiful moment of spiritual enlightenment for me.

After the healing session ended, Alannah asked my Higher Self,

So, what will Marcas notice in the future as a result of this blockage being gone?

My Higher Self is speaking at a raised level of consciousness to Alannah and tells her, *He'll see…the light. He'll see…more.*

Alannah expands on what my Higher Self is saying, *He will see more. How it really is. He hasn't been seeing how things really are?*

My Higher Self replies, *No.*

Alannah continues, *But now he will be able to see things as they really are?*

My Higher Self explains, *His emotions were too strong because his neck was blocked. And now he will see!*

Alannah prompts for the status of the healing session by the angels,

Excellent. Can you continue to scan his body and see if there's anything else out of balance in terms of health or harmony in all of his physical, mental, spiritual, and emotional bodies? What do you want to tell him? Are you finished with that?

My Higher Self responds to Alannah by confirming that the angels working on healing the blockage in my neck were done.

This limited, yet intense, experience with Reiki healing has opened my eyes to the healing power within us all. I am not saying Reiki healing cured all my ailments. I can say Reiki was responsible for healing the annoying pain in my upper right arm.

Visions of Trauma In A Past Life

Looking for hidden traumatic memories from your past lives is one of the main themes in Maria Elena's Module Two. Hidden, traumatic memories from your past lives can be especially difficult to find. Maria Elena says one of the most successful ways to find past life trauma is to be guided to these past lives by trained therapists. She goes on to explain how some memories can fragment your soul. She states pieces of your soul wander off to safety, to who knows where, until you have consciously taken the time to find these hidden, traumatic memories and heal them. When you find out what they are and work on healing them, you can rejoin your soul in this current life. You will begin to feel whole in your mind, body, and soul. You feel loved. You become aware and yearn to learn more about your higher purpose in life. Your ego is reduced to nothing and you will migrate toward freely helping others.

Now that you have lightened up in the first and second modules of Maria Elena's process, you are ready to move on to Module Three. You accept you are more than a physical body.

You are a sacred being. Your elevated consciousness transcends the physical world and is eternal. You do not die.

At this level of higher consciousness, you work on self-realization in the broadest sense of the word. Your whole self is made up of mind, body, and soul. You are more aware of your Higher Self and start actively exploring. You acknowledge the existence of spiritual dimensions and start reflecting on the more divine aspects of God. You learn that, as sacred beings, we have more power to change the way people on Earth perceive reality than we were taught in our current life.

TAPE 3

As I continue listening to the QHHT visions recorded on Tape 3, it becomes obvious to me that my Higher Self has a far greater perspective of reality than my current reincarnation on Earth.

Alannah asks my Higher Self,

So, what are you going to work on next?

My Higher Self responds,

Maybe his soul needs to be woken up a little bit.

Alannah seems intrigued by this idea.

Can you help him wake up your soul a little bit?

My Higher Self answers, *Yeah.*

What is the difference between the Higher Self and the Soul?

Your soul is your larger existence, the consciousness that is evolving and is at a certain stage of awakening, based on all of your life experiences. I, the Higher Self, am the awakened one, the aware one, the part of you that still knows God. Your soul is the sum total of all the jigsaw pieces you have collected (so to speak) and I am the whole completed puzzle.

You become me as you become all that is. I am the completed one, the bigger picture guiding you forth. Your soul is the sum total so far, it has wounds to heal from past lives, gifts to uncover from them too, and much to learn and integrate. I hope this is sufficiently clear for you to understand.[113]

…Confusing. I think the soul keeps getting reincarnated and the Higher Self is a spiritual guide we all have that understands the big picture and guides the soul until the soul becomes one with the Higher Self in a higher spiritual dimension.

My Higher Self reports they have found the problem with my soul that needs fixing.

There we go! It is all wrapped in gray and it's bursting out now. It is bursting out in big, colorful rays. Yeah! I don't

---

113   'The difference between our higher self and our soul – Jodi-Anne's Insights into Peace and Happiness,' Jodie Smith, jodi-annemsmith.com, (22 July 2015).

know where the gray came from.

Alannah encourages my Higher Self,

Just keep removing it. Just keep blasting it. You are powerful. You're very wise. You are love, you are loved. Use your full power.

My Higher Self reports what is happening,

I think it's protection. It's going to ... spreading it, spreading, spreading out. Yeah, that's nice. It doesn't need all that protection. Get rid of that. Yeah. It's better now.

Alannah replies, *Wonderful.*

The conversation continues, as transcribed directly from the QHHT session recording…

Marcas: *It opened up channels to all the rest of my body. So, I might be able to self-heal now because I filled it with the white light. Yeah, it was all wrapped up.*

Alannah: *What's all wrapped up?*

Marcas: *My soul was all wrapped up. It was protecting itself.*

Alannah: *I see.*

Marcas: *So, we could do that.*

Alannah: *So, can you help him be protected if he needs*

protection and now be protective when he's safe and knows it, feels the difference, and empowers him so he has confidence and has complete knowledge and belief in himself?

Marcas: *Yeah.*

Alannah: *How can you help him with this?*

Marcas: *By releasing the light.*

Alannah: *Releasing the light.*

Alannah: *So, can you take him back to the very, very first incarnation where he needed protection? Going back, back in time. Back in time when something significant was happening that you want Marcas to know about and experience. Tell me when you're aware of it.*

Marcas: *Hooded figures. Ku Klux Klan. Yeah. That's when I needed protection.*

Alannah: *And so, who are you in that lifetime? Does it feel like you have a body?*

Marcas: *I don't see myself. But I know I need protecting.*

Alannah: *And what's happening as you watch the Ku Klux Klan figures? What color were they?*

Marcas: *Just kind of dark blue or something. Kind of greyish blue. Thanks. Yeah, but they're just standing there like they are waiting.*

Alannah: *Who are they waiting for?*

Marcas: *I don't know. They just think…they have it all figured out. Yeah. They are such a small, small group. Not very many of them. They don't understand anything.*

Alannah: *They don't understand anything*

Marcas: *No. I don't know why. I don't know why.*

Alannah: *Let's close that scene….*

Alannah closes this disturbing vision from one of my previous lives by gently saying,

Just drift and flow to another important scene in the lifetime we're watching with the hooded figures moving backward or forward …Arriving there now. Where are you?

My above reincarnation memory seems to relate to an earlier scene in my QHHT session when Alannah found out that my vitiligo is a soul contract[114] designed to show others the fact that skin color is not important. I now know skin color is not important to the spiritual enlightenment of our soul on Earth and in Heaven.

Again, my Higher Self has to speak for me because I am out of my league with this conversation. I did not understand the following conversation until I spent a lot of time researching and reading the meaning and use of crystals to heal and expand your

---

114   Crawford, H. (2019, March 23). 11 Facts About Soul Contracts, Agreements & Debts. *Numerologist.Com.* https://numerologist.com/spiritual-growth/soul-contracts/

spiritual awareness.

My Higher Self replies,

It's all white and crystals are growing out of the snow. And that's it.

My Higher Self explains,

That's where the crystals come from. They are coming from all white.

Alannah asks,

So what do you do when you see the crystals of white?

This scene is so foreign to my conscious mind, that I tell her,

I don't know, just passing through that's what I see.

Alannah asks,

Do you have a body?

I reply,

No, it's just my soul.

Alannah said,

Drifting and floating...

I said,

I am calm and just soaking it all in, Yeah.

Alannah prompts me further,

Wonderful. Back with the crystals with white light...

Until the QHHT session, I had never thought much about the spiritual powers of crystals and the energy generated from various colored crystal stones. I wondered why there was so much emphasis on the healing power of crystals in astrology and holistic healing methods such as Reiki. My scientific mind asks how anyone could make a strange claim about crystals having healing powers.

When I was in a hypnotized state, I had several visions of crystals in the shape of pyramids. Reviewing the session transcripts regarding crystals was not easy because I still didn't understand how crystals can heal you. Yet, my Higher Self had no problem explaining this phenomenon when I was under hypnosis.

During the Reiki session, the brightness of the energy healing different parts of my body was blinding.

Alannah asked,

Can you dim down the brightness or put sunglasses on so the energies or entities behind the white light will be shown to you?

I struggled to respond,

It's uh...Almost like a headband of crystals and crystalline crystals ...

Again, I am guided by my spirit guides and Higher Self at a point in writing this book to a passage from Candice Sanderson's amazing book of visions. The passage helps me understand how the vision of a divine healing headband with several different colored crystals and the powerful rays of our sun can both be used to heal.[115]

I had a 'knowing' during the dream, similar to what sometimes occurs in the messages, and I knew the changes in the sun's rays were altering Earth's elements through the gemstones. I wondered why. I recalled the dream in full detail when I woke up the next morning. The sun's transformation into a lotus flower with a thousand petals puzzled me. Why a lotus flower, and why such a specific number of petals? I found an article online entitled 'What Is the Thousand-Petaled Lotus?' This lotus is said to represent the seventh or crown chakra. (Chakras are swirling disks of energy located near the spine; the crown chakra is located at the top of the head.) ...

October 19, 2013. The sun is another source of its own. The energy emanating from the sun is powerful and

---

115   Sanderson, Candice. The Reluctant Messenger-Tales from Beyond Belief: An ordinary person's extraordinary journey into the unknown (p. 106). Clark Press. Kindle Edition.

divided into separate rays. The different rays from the sun represent different levels and types of energy. This energy goes throughout the universe to the areas where those particular frequencies are needed. There are humans on the Earth plane who can recognize the separate energies and are able to channel them to where they will be of greatest benefit...

There is a new type of lightworker on the Earth who is able to gather these subtle energies and send them deep into the core of Mother Earth for healing. These lightworkers are beacons, drawing specific subtle frequencies into their personal energy fields, and then releasing the energies deep into the Earth. These are specific energy frequencies targeted for healing your beloved Mother Earth. Just as crystals store and amplify energy in our three-dimensional world, so did the gemstone clusters in the dream. They operated as magnets that attracted the energy from the divergent rays. When the rays struck their surfaces, they infused them with a new set of energy frequencies, which caused them to awaken and come to life. Each gemstone has specific healing properties. The divergent rays activated these innate elements which resulted in a multitude of restorative energies.[116]

---

116   Ibid, pp. 106-108.

Visions of Crystals

Maria Elena Mexia's Module Four of Healing requires you to reach a very high level of consciousness before you can start exploring the powers each of us has but are not aware of.

Once in a great while, the Creator grants us the opportunity for a rare glimpse into the inner workings of Nature. The mysteries of the spiritual world have remained hidden for thousands of years. ...[117]

In general, it can be stated that our understanding of consciousness is not broad enough yet. We have been strapped by the current laws of physics and the belief we are not divine and could never reach our true potential as light beings inside a physical body.

Many believe that starting in 2022, we have entered the Age of Aquarius. This age in the astrological cosmic cycle of time will allow us to reach a higher level of spiritual awareness than ever before.[118]

The guidance from my Higher Self helped me get a great start on healing burdensome, traumatic issues with my physical, mental, and spiritual body. I am now able to see through my

117   'Amazon.com: The Spiritual World', Documentary on Prime Video, Spiritual Awakening S1 E1 2020. The Speaker is Mitchell Gibson. The Message Company Presents The International Conference on Science & Consciousness.

118   'Aquarius Season', Conscious Reminder, https://consciousreminder.com/2022/01/21/aquarius-season-2022-through-dates-all-the-cosmic-support-you-need/

superconscious mind's eye. In just one QHHT session, I experienced going through all four levels of Maria Elena's *Four Modules of Healing* process.

With my inner energy channels unblocked, I could explore an expanded reality at a higher level of consciousness.

Entering this higher, spiritual dimension during my QHHT session was shocking to me. It was difficult for me to understand what the following QHHT session vision meant. I tried following Allanah's rule, *Just tell me what you see...*

Crystals are used to create brand new souls for reincarnation to Earth or other planets in the universe.

The technique used to create souls: You focus a beam of white light at the top of a pyramid-shaped prism. Once inside the pyramid, a white blob is formed on what looks like a wire hanging from the very top of the pyramid peak — like a lightning rod to collect intense energy to a specific spot. The focused energy in the pyramid becomes a white blob and segments into three body sections. It looks like the start of a snowman.

We all start out so clean!

Everywhere else is darkness....

There is white snow on the ground and it is filling up with little black sprouts in freshly fallen snow. You have to keep on the path of the freshly fallen snow, even if it has a few black sprouts in it now. If you go off the path, you will fall into darkness.

Alannah tells me to follow the path. I do not want to go. I suddenly see we are in a brand new world full of love but it is just full of volcanoes and rocks.

I am now in a brand new world.

Alannah states, *New worlds and they start out white.*

I cannot go any further in this dream. I am being told by my Higher Self or spirit guides I just need to stay on the path. I show the new souls the path to this new world.

Alannah asks me what I look like in this vision. I tell her I have taken on the shape of a brand-new soul. I am just three white blobs of dough on top of each other. I don't know how I reach the other souls to show them the way to the new world. My spirit guides will not let me go any further.

I explain, *It's probably too complicated.*

Alannah asks my Higher Self/spirit guides to please show me more.

I start to see a bunch of bodies. It is like they are all in outer space and there are stars.

There is a row of empty bodies. I think my snowman soul body goes in one of them. The bodies are just empty shells until a brand new, pure soul enters them.

Alannah asks what the empty shells represent.

They're like little space pods ready to go somewhere. You just enter them and you go to…You go somewhere in the universe. The space pods are three-dimensional.

That is what they were showing me. I was being shown I was just a white, segmented blob. I was a freshly created soul in another dimension (heaven?). I was just the innards of the empty shell.

Alannah asks,

Do they put a soul in there? Are they like cars or something?

I reply,

The whole body is the soul, It's just like white dough. It's just segmented into three different parts of your body but it's all just blank. It's all clean. Nice and clean.

My Higher Self, again, shows me all the stars in the universe.

I get the feeling they are showing me where all these freshly made and packaged souls travel in the universe. The space pod 'bodies' are at the edge of the universe waiting until the dough fills them up.

It's a protective shell. Sometimes it's a long way to where they have to go because they have to go in three-dimensional space to get to their destination. For the soul, it's far. Things all of a sudden are far.

I don't know. That's just what I see.

Alannah asks me where the brand-new souls come from and I just start repeating what I had already said about the white light forming blobs inside crystal pyramids.

Alannah wants me to continue the progression of the soul creation and transportation process but I tell her,

I don't think I want to…I'm tired…It's too much. Too, too much…It's a lot of energy.

Alannah starts bringing me back into consciousness and we discuss the lessons learned from the very last vision of my QHHT journey.

I am happy with the messages I received. I believe my Higher Self/spirit guides were telling me I must be a humble guide on this Earth and show people the way to stay on the path toward spiritual enlightenment and toward the love God has to offer.

Yeah. I am some kind of helper along the way. That's cool! I am positive energy. I don't want to think ahead…it might set me off on some tangent. I don't want it…I just want to be clean and clear and do what they tell me to do.

Alannah told me,

Dolores (Cannon) had the Higher Self recede into the past but sometimes I have the Higher Self merge with the current self. Is this okay or do you want me to do it the traditional way?

I told Alannah I was not very interested in my previous lives.

I said,

*I got pretty far in this life...I'm farther than I was in my
past lives where it was just, you know, ignorance and
soaking it all in.*

My Higher Self and spirit guides chose to show me one more
powerful vision as Alannah read a final script to pull me gently
out of my hypnotic state.

My last QHHT vision was not on the QHHT recording I
received because I had it while Alannah was bringing me out
of my hypnotic state. It was a very powerful message. I believe I
finally understand what it means...

I witnessed Jesus come out onto a white, billowy cloud
bathed, all around, in bright, white light.

After I had gone home, I started reading Candice Sanderson's
book, The Reluctant Messenger — Tales From Beyond Belief: An
Ordinary Person's Extraordinary Journey Into The Unknown at
the beginning of 2021. I was desperately trying to find others
who might have experienced the same journey of spiritual
enlightenment I was just starting on. I found out Candice
Sanderson kept a remarkably detailed journal of all her visions
and dreams over the years.

She had also written a very informative, easy-to-read book
about how she began her spiritual enlightenment journey...and
she was still alive. I immediately contacted her through email.

I now share one of the emails I sent her explaining my last

vision of meeting Jesus Christ. I have never had a vision like this in any of the previous dreams I have blogged about.

Here is the email I just sent Alannah, my QHHT session therapist, to show you how close your visions are to mine.

I am still trying to figure out the last vision I had in my QHHT session where I saw Christ come out into an all-white platform in outer space to witness a great event.

Jesus has auburn-colored hair. I feel welcome there.

The vision then shows me some very tall, white-robed, blond-haired figures lined up on either side of a path made of clouds. The path leads up to a billowy, white platform.

A young couple appears in standard wedding attire (white, flowing wedding dress, and black tux). They have dark brunette hair.

They run between the rows of tall, white-robed figures up to the platform and stare at the great black expanse in front of them, speckled with stars.

I find it interesting the details of the hair I noticed. It was as if humans had the darkest colored hair, then came Jesus with his auburn-colored hair, and then came the very tall, white-robed figures with blond hair.

I have done some research on ascension into heaven or to the source. There is mention of very tall, blond-haired beings of the Aryan race fitting into the ascension hierarchy. There are also pictures of Jesus on YouTube with auburn hair. It is as if Jesus was the medium between humans and the higher race of heavenly beings. I have had several tall entity dreams ranging from the sands of Egypt to a locker room in Heaven [Ref. Appendix 1].

There are also people referencing fields of flowers in YouTube videos. On the way to heaven, it is not uncommon to stop in a field of flowers of great expanse. It is also not unusual to see very tall beings of a more heavenly race than humans....

This whole journey into the metaphysical realm started on September 27th, 2020, when a voice in my head told me to read a book called Journey of Souls. This book outlined, in detail, the commonality in the visions of people who were mildly hypnotized by the author, Michael Newton, using his Life Between Lives (LBL) hypnosis technique. I started noticing dreams I have had and blogged about, months and even years before matching my dreams with Michael Newton's clients' visions when they were under mild hypnosis.

I wanted to compare some of the dreams I have had and relate them, not only to the cases outlined in Journey of Souls but to other authors as well. Specifically, Dolores Cannon, Candice Sanderson, and David Rippy.

Listening to your podcasts and reading your books, I am now thinking Jesus showed me we humans are now ready to take on a journey to explore the universe. We have now graduated to a point where we can be change drivers ... to

drive positive energy and ideas across the universe. My
vision showed me how much faith and love Jesus has in us!

There was no doubt in my mind that, entering the QHHT session, I had become quite the rebel by constantly resisting listening to spiritual guidance in my previous afterlife dreams. I knew I was also being defiant in my previous after-lives. I was having a lot of fun trying to understand how the real afterlife operated by going to places in this realm I was not supposed to go and explore.

There were dreams I had where I was connected to a prohibited, higher energy level in the cosmos or I was somewhere in the afterlife I was not supposed to go. These prohibited, super high-energy locations stretched my mind beyond what we currently know.

A couple of times visiting these high-energy locations shook my physical body to the core.[119],[120],[121] My powerful dreams were a wake-up call like Scrooge had before the three Spirits of Christmas came to see him in A Christmas Carol by Charles Dickens.[122]

119   Major, M. 'A Dream that Shook Me to the Core', *Religion of One* (09-24-2013). https://relofone.blogspot.com/2013/09/09-242013-dream-that-shook-me-to-core.html

120   Major, M. 'I Am Becoming A Bit of A Pest in Other Worldly Dreams', *Religion of One* (7-07-2018). https://relofone.blogspot.com/2018/07/07-07-2018-i-am-becoming-bit-of-pest-in.html

121   Major, M. 'Another Dream Of Ghosts When Overtired', *Religion of One* (01-11-2020). https://relofone.blogspot.com/2020/01/01-11-2020-another-dream-of-ghosts-in.html

122   Ebenezer Scrooge. (2022). In *Wikipedia*. https://en.wikipedia.org/w/index.php?title=Ebenezer_Scrooge&oldid=1128783591

My defiant attitude came out as I freely floated to some very strange, out-of-this-world locations during my QHHT session. I laughed when I had the vision of crystal pyramids in a field of snow. Alannah asked why I had laughed after telling her about the crystal pyramid vision I was having.

I said, *Because I don't think I am supposed to be here.*

Alannah tried to move me forward in this crystal pyramid vision, but I was mentally exhausted. I did not want to go any further.

Chapter 7: Completing The Puzzle

INTRODUCTION

I have described my maiden voyage into a metaphysical world. Getting out there and experiencing what others would rather watch happen from their comfy couches has always been my preference when it comes to sports and other physical activities. Experiencing spiritual activities was not high on my to-do list, however.

Access to the spirit realm requires a quantum leap into the currently unexplained capabilities within each of us. I validated the claim our superconscious mind could travel to a spiritual dimension when I got out there and experienced my maiden voyage into my superconscious mind's eye with Alannah's gentle guidance. She guided me to a spiritual dimension where I saw visions of Mary, Jesus, and other powerful spirits. It is possible to explore your past lives, get the answers you are looking for to help you in your current existence and discover hints of what your future existence in the afterlife will look like. I experienced wise words and visions from beyond this world during my QHHT therapy session.

Entering a somnambulistic hypnotic state places your mind in a low-energy state. It took me over fifteen years to figure out that a low-energy state of mind was when I could see my clearest visions of ghosts. I needed to be guided by a highly trained QHHT therapist to see beyond ghosts.

Each person's view of reality is based on the tools they have acquired to view their reality. My view of reality has expanded beyond the limits of this three-dimensional world. I had to start listening and looking for subtle hints along the way. It took a great effort for me to initially see a reality beyond our Earthly bounds ... a metaphysical reality. I had to learn how to use senses within me that I did not know I had and learn a lot of new words to define metaphysical concepts I only had glimpses of in my dreams. Many reputable institutions are ready to help you with proven tools needed to gain insight into your eternal soul (e.g. The Monroe Institute[123], QHHT[124], and LBL[125] certified therapists, etc.).

A lot of people are just trying to survive, day to day. Many people choose to believe in only what has been written in books

---

123   *Experiential Expanded Consciousness Meditation Programs and Research*. (n.d.). The Monroe Institute. Retrieved December 26, 2022, from https://www.monroeinstitute.org/

124   *QHHT {Quantum Healing Hypnosis Technique} Official Training*. (2020, November 17). https://www.qhhtofficial.com/

125   Michael Newton, 'Life Between Lives', *Newton Institute*, https://www.newtoninstitute.org/life-between-lives/

for established religions. I chose to ignore most of the books written for established religions and resisted looking into the possibility of an alternative path to spiritual enlightenment because the concepts were not logical and not scientifically proven... until I heard a voice in my head telling me to read a specific metaphysical book.

I thought nothing substantial had been written about metaphysical concepts. The truth is I had not even taken a look at what had been published on metaphysical subjects and phenomena. There is a wealth of books, e-books, and videos available on metaphysical concepts and metaphysical history. If you do not know the search words to use to look up all the metaphysical information at your fingertips you will remain in the dark. That is why I sprinkled this book with definitions I had to look up the meaning of. It will save you a few steps in your spiritual enlightenment journey.

To complete my writing of this book, I had to reign in my unquenchable thirst for more knowledge about each metaphysical subject I discovered and only concentrate on learning what was already published on the metaphysical ideas my dreams and QHHT session visions were showing me.

The first part of this book explained my background. My goal was to try and convince you I had the right training to research and write this book. My previous broad education and complex, technical jobs trained me to research and collect known facts about how business processes work and how they could be improved with new technology. The metaphysical keywords and phrases I needed to categorize and analyze the strange dreams and QHHT session visions I had required a lot of research and analysis.

By looking for repeating patterns in my strange dreams and visions, I was able to categorize all the strange dreams I had blogged about by type. There were dreams about my past, present, and future. There were dreams where I visited parallel worlds and there were dreams about my afterlife experiences. My dreams were impossible visions of reality, according to most of the currently accepted scientific principles.

After connecting all the puzzle pieces together, I now had a broader view of reality. I was able to validate my strange dreams and visions to published, metaphysical research papers and similar experiences published by other people. My view of reality was now spiritually enlightened. Spiritual Enlightenment was something I thought I would never understand.

Never say never.

I am now aware of a whole ocean of metaphysical knowledge available to explore and understand. My research has revealed our immortal soul's reality can span thousands of years on Earth. My mind-bending dreams and QHHT visions weaved through the past to show me glimpses of some of the previous lives I have experienced on Earth and in the afterlife.

It is still confusing for me to process the sudden visions and voices in my head. In the early morning of September 11, 2022,

Eric Lucas paid me a visit in my dream. I have had very few dreams where there is such a strong and clear vision of a person I know who passed away. When I saw him, my mind was thinking he was still alive. Eric had passed away exactly one year earlier on September 11th, 2021.

In my vision, Eric caught on fast that I was confused. He tried to have an intelligent conversation with me. It didn't work... Hey, I was sleeping!

Eric said, *Anyway... Finish your book.*

I found out at his memorial that he was working on writing another book when he died.

I am convinced there is an undeniable core of spiritual existence in all of us. My soul experienced many previous lives and has quite a lot to show and tell me. All I need to do is look and listen.

This book was not written to change your religious beliefs. It was written because I wanted to share my powerful afterlife dreams and visions with you and explain to you what conclusions I have come to. I do hope this encourages you to continue believing in an afterlife.

My final discussion in this book will examine who I think Archangel Metatron is. I will relate who I believe Metatron is and what he is responsible for, as well as some of my personal experiences, dreams, and visions. Historical accounts of Metatron from various sources are also discussed.

I have learned our eternal souls are threads weaving in and out of time and space on our spiritual journey toward being One with God.

IT WASN'T ME...

Most of my QHHT therapy session visions were not in my control. I now believe that my QHHT visions were displayed to me by Archangel Metatron. My visions were a summary of the many wonderful things Metatron has accomplished and the actions he has taken to fulfill his current responsibilities.

He wanted to show me who he is and what he has done.

Most of my time during the QHHT session was spent concentrating on pushing my limited amount of energy toward keeping alert and aware of all the visions Archangel Metatron chose to show me and verbalizing what I saw to Alannah. I had never tried to keep up with a spirit bird flying away from me in a vision in my mind before. Alannah captured all I told her on three digital recordings for later review. At one point during the QHHT session, I noticed my feet were getting cold. Alannah quickly covered them with another blanket and said,

That's okay. It takes a lot of energy to follow your visions.

When I started reviewing my pre-QHHT session chakra alignment/cleansing recording and my three QHHT session recordings, in earnest, on 05-11-2021, I heard a voice in my head say,

Finally! I want to show you who I am!

At the start of the QHHT session, I asked Alannah to not hold back because of my lack of experience in the QHHT process. I wanted to experience the *full meal deal*. I got what I asked for. I was shown all the splendor of a very real and complex spiritual realm.

Note: I am not paying too much attention to whether I use Archangel Metatron or just Metatron as his name. They are both the same figure, a being of immense power, in my eyes, and I have great respect for the entity, regardless of the way I spell his name.

Definition of Archangel

An angel of high rank.

In traditional Christian angelology, a being of the eighth order of the ninefold celestial hierarchy.[126]

An archangel is an angel of high rank. The word archangel itself is usually associated with the Abrahamic religions, but beings that are very similar to archangels are found in a number of religious traditions.[127]

Melanie Beckler is a prolific, insightful author. She also has many YouTube videos on all subjects touching the metaphysical

126   Powered by <u>Oxford Languages</u>, <u>Bing Translator</u>.
127   Archangel. (2022). In *Wikipedia*. <u>https://en.wikipedia.</u> <u>org/w/index.php?title=Archangel&oldid=1129130593</u>

realm. Melanie states angels are in a different dimension than we are. We can learn to sense, hear, and even see angels when our minds are in a more relaxed state. [128,129]

HISTORICAL ACCOUNTS OF THE NAME METATRON

There are historical accounts of two Metatrons. One of the two historical Metatrons is defined as a primordial entity and the other Metatron is the one mentioned in the Book of Enoch. One idea describes Enoch as taken by God and transformed into Metatron, in this passage from Genesis:

Enoch walked with God; then he was no more because God took him away.[130]

Enoch ascended into heaven and became known as Archangel Metatron.[131] This viewpoint is not shared by all religions. Most Christian religions do not recognize the Archangel Metatron at all.

I am going with the flow and recognizing Archangel Metatron as real. Besides being told by my pre-QHHT chakra cleansing and alignment therapist, Heather, I have read references to Metatron in several well-established religions and lesser-known

128   Melanie Beckler (Director). (2012, April 3). *Archangel Michael Angel Message, Clear Cleanse & Lift Meditation.* https://www.youtube.com/watch?v=EJjLIl7NMk0.
129   'Melanie Beckler, Author, Angelic Channel, Ascension Way Shower', ask-angels.com.
130   Genesis 5:24 NIV.
131   Metatron. (2022). In *Wikipedia.* https://en.wikipedia.org/w/index.php?title=Metatron&oldid=1129213267

cults dating back to ancient Egypt.[132]

Jewish myths and legends regard Metatron as the greatest of angels. Metatron has many responsibilities as God's mediator with men.[133]

The story of Moses leading the Israelites out of the punishing desert is well known. Moses split the Red Sea in half with his heavenly staff. The Israelites walked to their new home using the path left by splitting the sea in two. There is also a reference in the Exodus story, mentioned in the Bible and the Torah, where God sends a mysterious, unnamed angel to manifest as Moses and help guide the Israelites out of the desert. Some people believe the angel sent down from heaven to manifest as Moses was Metatron.[134] Did Metrtron greet me at Heaven's Gate with a golden staff as mentioned in a QHHT vision I had (see Ch.6)?

I was never taught about Metatron in Sunday school. The possibility of Metatron manifesting as Moses and guiding the Israelites out of the desert was discovered after I felt I was gently encouraged, in my mind, to watch two recent Expedition Unknown episodes all about Moses[135] and the story of how Moses guided the Israelites out of the desert of Egypt but

132   Ibid.
133   Metatron | Archangel & Description | Britannica. (n.d.). Retrieved December 26, 2022, from https://www.britannica.com/topic/Metatron
134   Who Was the Angel Who Guided Moses During the Exodus? (n.d.). Learn Religions. Retrieved December 26, 2022, from https://www.learnreligions.com/angel-who-guided-moses-124031
135   Mysteries of Moses. (n.d.). Discovery. Retrieved December 26, 2022, from https://www.discovery.com/shows/expedition-un-known/episodes/7a2a/mysteries-of-moses

did not bring them to the Promised Land. On the show, Josh Gates follows the historical evidence of the Exodus led by Moses, starting from Mt. Sinai where Moses received the Ten Commandments. Moses angrily threw the stone tablets, on which the Ten Commandments were written, onto the ground when he came down from Mt. Sinai and saw that his followers had abandoned his guidance from God and were worshiping a golden calf idol.[136] I discovered the link between Metatron and Moses at the same time I was researching further on the internet about the life of Moses.

Moses had an anger problem and did not always do what God asked him to do. It is said God refused to allow him into the Promised Land to punish Moses for not having complete faith in God and not doing exactly what God told him to do. Joshua, son of Nun became responsible for bringing the Israelites to their Promised Land after Moses was punished.[137] Moses was pretty far down in the branches of Adam and Eve's family tree but he was a descendant.[138]

There are two Enochs in Adam and Eve's extended family tree. Cain, Abel, and Seth were the three sons of Adam and Eve. Cain had a son named Enoch. This is not the Enoch who became

136   *Golden calf ¶ – Wikipedia.* (n.d.). Retrieved December 25, 2022, from https://en.wikipedia.org/wiki/Golden_calf

137   *God shows Moses the Promised Land – Catholic Courier.* (n.d.). Retrieved December 21, 2022, from https://catholiccourier.com/articles/god-shows-moses-the-promised-land/

138   *What is the order of Adam and Eve's descendants to Moses?* (n.d.). Answers. Retrieved December 26, 2022, from https://www.answers.com/Q/What_is_the_order_of_Adam_and_Eve's_descendants_to_Moses

Metatron. The Enoch who was considered the same person as Metatron was the son of Jared. Jared was a descendant of Adam and Eve's son, Seth.

Seth's brother Cain was seriously enraged when he found out God had favored the gift his brother, Abel, gave God. Cain ended up murdering his brother Abel out of pure spite.[139] There were some hot-tempered offspring in Adam and Eve's family tree!

I think I might have experienced a sample of the hot tempers within Adam and Eve's family tree in a dream I had. When proofreading this book, I realized the dream I once had discussed an entity whose name was Set. Perhaps I was not hearing what was said in my dream correctly. I do have a hearing problem with soft-sounding words ending in *th* and other soft consonant sounds. The name in my dream could easily have been Seth. Was the Seth in my dream the son of Adam and Eve and was Metatron (Enoch) a descendant of the Seth in my dream?

The lady I saw in Set's home in my dream warned me that Set would not like it when he found out I was snooping around his private quarters. If the lady in my dream had a soft-spoken voice, she may have said the name Seth and not Set. I did not want Seth to hold a grudge because I said Seth's name wrong in the dream I blogged about. He already yelled at me once in that dream and it shook me to the core.

All these names relating Metatron to Enoch and in turn, to

---

139   Cain and Abel. (2022). In *Wikipedia.* https://en.wikipedia. org/w/index.php?title=Cain_and_Abel&oldid=1127802097

Adam and Eve, could be knowledge of my ancient soul family buried deep in my soul that only comes out when I dream about my past. Even if I was not hard of hearing in real life, it is understandable how I could become confused with the names Set and Seth. I just happened to be reading a book series called _The Kane Chronicles_ by Rick Riordan with an evil character named Set. The confusion in the names of Kane versus Cain and Set versus Seth may have been enough to jog my subconscious mind to show me a dream about one of my ancient, rebellious past lives and my encounter with Seth (Ref. _https://relofone.blogspot.com/2018/07/07-07-2018-i-am-becoming-bit-of-pest-in.html_).

I do not think Seth was evil in Adam and Eve's lineage. You would think I would have no problem with hearing in dreams, but the issue with my hearing is more complicated than you might think. Your brain physically stops trying to listen for sounds it cannot hear after a while.[140]

HOW METATRON RELATES TO MY DREAMS AND VISIONS

In Chapter 5 of this book, under Pre-QHHT Practice Exercises, there was a subtle hint that Archangel Metatron was directly communicating with me in my visions. While going through the QHHT exercises that Alannah emailed to me on 10-17-2020, I had a vision of a man on a park bench wearing an old, red velvet smoking jacket.

---

140   BC-HIS, J. J. J. (2019, July 4). _You Hear With Your Brain, Not Your Ears | Hearing Health Blog._ Selective Hearing Centers. https://myselectivehearing.com/you-hear-with-your-brain-not-your-ears/

He told me, *Remember the word velvet.*

Fast forward to one of my very first QHHT session visions with a scene of me as a small child in pauper's clothing. I entered an empty throne room, with deep red, velvet curtains. The scene I was in was described back in Chapter 6, Tape 1 of this book. In the throne room, there was also...

...a shrine or throne embossed with ornate gold designs and trimmed with the same deep red velvet as the curtains.

The deep red velvet material of the throne room was also the same as Metatron's smoking jacket in my vision two weeks earlier.

In my QHHT vision, I remember being in awe of this beautiful throne room filled with luxurious décor and also feeling a little puzzled because there was no one in this beautiful room.

The keyword 'velvet' helped me fit the puzzle pieces of my two seemingly unrelated visions together, even when the two visions occurred weeks apart.

Definition of Velvet

A closely woven fabric of silk, cotton, or nylon, that has a thick short pile on one side.[141]

Metatron was the person I saw in my QHHT practice exercise

---

141   *Oxford Languages | The Home of Language Data.* (n.d.). Retrieved December 26, 2022, from https://languages.oup.com/

vision on the park bench wearing the deep red, velvet smoking jacket. The empty throne room with the deep red, velvet décor was Metatron's throne room. The definition of velvet is a closely woven fabric of silk, cotton, or nylon. I learned I am closely woven into Metatron's soul family. The words and visions I received from Archangel Metatron are deep in meaning. I am sure there is even more meaning to the word velvet that I have not discovered yet. I could even speculate that the reference to silk, cotton, and nylon pretty much covers the period of my QHHT visions dating from the modern fabric of today's nylon to the cotton slave era and back to the time Pythagoras traveled along the Silk Road[142] trade route. This was how he learned about all the new ideas from several diverse cultures.

I found one source on the internet stating that Metatron clothes himself in the finest, most dazzling garments designed by God.

The Holy One (YHWH) also made Metatron a throne and curtain like His own and put them at the door to the Seventh Hall of Heaven.[143]

My practice QHHT vision of Metatron and my QHHT session vision of Metatron's throne are in line with this source's statement of Metatron being dressed in dazzling garments

---

142   *The Silk Road | National Geographic Society.* (n.d.). Retrieved December 26, 2022, from https://education.nationalgeographic.org/resource/silk-road

143   *Is Metatron in the Bible?* (n.d.). Galactic Federation Of Light. Retrieved December 25, 2022, from https://www.galacticfederationoflight.com/blogs/consciousness/is-metatron-bible

designed by God and having a throne room in heaven made by God.

Now I am beginning to believe the whole QHHT vision with the guards in a medieval castle and the throne room was not on Earth. According to the source in the footnote, I may have been witnessing Archangel Metatron's throne room in the Seventh Hall of Heaven after Archangel Metatron had already ascended into heaven.[144]

The fact I was able to describe the detailed, golden embroidery trim on the ornate throne and deep red velvet curtains, in my vision, proves to me it was one of Archangel Metatron's QHHT visions. I am not a very detail-oriented person in my clothing selections. There has been no extra effort, on my part, to stop wearing casual blue jeans and polos to become more fashionably dressed like Metatron was.

METATRON'S RESPONSIBILITIES

This section reviews some of the responsibilities Archangel Metatron has and why he may have chosen to show me these specific responsibilities during my QHHT session.

---

144   Ibid. https://www.galacticfederationoflight.com/blogs/consciousness/is-metatron-bible

Metatron is the Scribe for God

According to the Talmud[145], Archangel Metatron is considered the highest of angels and was allowed to sit by God because of his function as the Heavenly Scribe, writing down the merits of Israel, just as Thoth[146] was the Egyptian scribe.

Definition of Talmud

The body of Jewish civil and ceremonial law and legend comprising the Mishnah and the Gemara. There are two versions of the Talmud: the Babylonian Talmud (which dates from the 5th century AD but includes earlier material) and the earlier Palestinian or Jerusalem Talmud.

One of Archangel Metatron's main responsibilities is to record all that has happened in our universe in the Akashic records. These historical records reside in the Etheric Plane.[147] He has direct access to everything that ever happened in the universe. The word *scribe* may be a misnomer since a lot is happening in the universe through the spoken word and visions. The written word is the most common definition of a scribe's function. The more modern definition of the word *record* could be valid for capturing speech, visions, and the written word.

145   *Meet Archangel Metatron, Angel of Life.* (n.d.). Learn Religions. Retrieved December 26, 2022, from https://www.learnreligions. com/meet-archangel-metatron-124083

146   *Thoth – Crystalinks.* (n.d.). Retrieved December 26, 2022, from https://www.crystalinks.com/thoth.html

147   Beckler, M. (2019, December 14). How to Access the Akashic Records For Knowledge, Healing and Growth. *Ask-Angels.Com.* https://www.ask-angels.com/spiritual-guidance/access-akashic-records/

Definition of Akashic

Akasha (ākāśa) is the Sanskrit word for aether, sky, or atmosphere.[148]

Other Responsibilities of Archangel Metatron

My QHHT session visions neatly fit into Metatron's responsibilities of sacred geometry, ascension, healing, and helping sensitive children (i.e. Indigo, Crystal, and Starseed children)[149] develop their special gifts to share with the world.[150]

Sacred Geometry

I witnessed strange visions of sacred geometry used to create the ancient castle I was in. It had spires reaching toward the heavens and ornate, Gothic architecture. As I traveled away from the ancient castle, I had a vision of a Mormon tabernacle where sacred geometry was also used to build this tabernacle. Sacred and symbolic meanings are defined by certain geometric shapes and the proportions used to build sacred geometric structures like tabernacles, churches, and mosques. The incorporation of specific geometric shapes into religious structures defines the

---

148   Rowell, L. (2015). *Music and Musical Thought in Early India.* University of Chicago Press. p. 48 https://press.uchicago.edu/ucp/books/book/chicago/M/bo3612674.html
149   Indigo, Crystal, & Starseed Children Characteristics. (n.d.). *Gaia.* Retrieved December 26, 2022, from https://www.gaia.com/article/indigo-crystal-starseed-children-characteristics
150   Dagny. (2014, November 16). Chakra Clearing with Reiki and Archangel Metatron. *Reiki Rays.* https://reikirays.com/16360/chakra-clearing-with-reiki-and-archangel-metatron/

structure as a sacred place to worship God.[151]

I floated into deep space. There was a vision of a small island with grey, folded, cardboard origami buildings . Beams of electromagnetic rays were shooting underneath these buildings from deep space. Then, a scary, fleshy root popped out from under the floating origami structures. The root poked me in my belly button.

Was this scary vision really just Metatron's way of showing me how he can create life from raw energy and basic constructs available in our Universe? The umbilical cord (now my belly button), in my mother's womb, did provide me with the raw energy needed to grow into a human being made out of flesh on Earth.

This was too strange for my mind to grasp, at the time, and I started becoming afraid. Alannah paused the session to pull me out of this disturbing vision so we could move on to other revealing visions.

My research, afterward, revealed that this strange vision Metatron chose to show me provided very specific details about how we are created in our universe. Sacred, folding geometric structures and magnetic energy are required to create life, according to my QHHT session vision.[152]

I recently found out that scientists have discovered how

151   Sacred geometry. (2022). In *Wikipedia*. https://en.wikipedia.org/w/index.php?title=Sacred_geometry&oldid=1126930187
152   Beckler, M. (2019, September 18). Sacred Geometry — Uncover The Secret Script of the Universe. *Ask-Angels.Com*. https://www.ask-angels.com/spiritual-guidance/sacred-geometry/

proteins fold in nature. It is a critical process. Notice the reference to the importance of *molecular origami* for the creation of life in the following excerpt. It is just like my QHHT session vision showed me.

> *Protein folding has been a grand challenge in biology for 50 years. An arcane form of molecular origami, its importance is hard to overstate. Most biological processes revolve around proteins and a protein's shape determines its function.*[153]

> *Thanks to Deep Mind's AlphaFold artificial intelligence network, scientists know the shapes of over two hundred million biological proteins used in over one million species … almost every known protein on our planet.*[154]

Scientists have also shown how something can be made of nothing but intense electromagnetic energy. The something they created was a hole. It rested itself on a two-dimensional (single molecular thickness) substrate of graphene. Anton Petrov has a YouTube video explaining the exact results of this remarkable experiment supporting the Schwinger Effect theory.[155] Metatron chose to show me the same power of creation electromagnetic

153   Major, M. 'How Angels Communicate When You Are Willing To Listen', *Religion of One* (03-20-2021). https://relofone.blogspot.com/2021/03/03-20-2021-how-angels-communicate-when.html

154   'The entire protein universe: AI predicts shape of nearly every known protein', *Nature*, https://www.nature.com/articles/d41586-022-02083-2#about-the-journal

155   Anton Petrov (Director). (2022, October 9). *Can Something Be Created Out of Nothing? Evidence For Schwinger Effect in Graphene.* https://www.youtube.com/watch?v=FTbOdzO8kqY

energy has in my QHHT vision over a year earlier than Anton Petrov's YouTube video!

There is a stained glass window on display in the *Museum of Church History and Art* in Salt Lake City, Utah depicting the founder of the Mormon religion kneeling in front of God and Jesus.

> *Joseph Smith said he received a vision in the spring of 1820 called the First Vision. Smith said that God the Father and his son Jesus Christ appeared to him and instructed him to join none of the existing churches because they were all wrong. ... Smith was seen by his followers as the modern-day prophet.*[156]

The figures of God and Jesus in the stained-glass depiction of Joseph Smith's First Vision are a lot taller than the image of Joseph Smith kneeling. The depiction of much taller, spiritual entities in heaven was also common in my QHHT session visions. Tall, holy entities in Heaven tend to be theomorphic.

Definition of Theomorphic

> *Having divine form: formed in the image of a deity: endued with a divine aspect.*[157]

---

156   Mormonism. (2022). In *Wikipedia*. https://en.wikipedia.org/w/index.php?title=Mormonism&oldid=1127434728

157   *Definition of THEOMORPHIC*. (n.d.). Retrieved December 28, 2022, from https://www.merriam-webster.com/dictionary/theomorphic

Fifth-dimensional beings. Theomorphic. Roughly eight to ten feet high. Sometimes taller.[158]

In my QHHT session vision, Mary appeared to be at least seven feet tall. Archangel Metatron was taller at about eight feet. The Aryan-looking entities I saw in my last vision were ten feet or taller and Jesus in my last QHHT session vision was taller and more glorious in stature than anyone else in my visions.

Ascension and Healing

It can be argued that Buddha, Jesus, Mother Mary, and Archangel Metatron are all ascended masters. They have all been recognized by God as exceptional in their spiritual advancement as humans on Earth. Their soul development reached a highly advanced state not requiring any further reincarnations. These masters now share their wisdom to help humans advance the spiritual development of their souls to a higher level.[159]

All the sacred geometry of the universe is defined in Metatron's Cube.[160]

Metatron's Cube is thirteen interconnecting circles with lines drawn between the circles into two pyramids, one upside

158   *The Spiritual World,* Documentary on Prime Video, 'Spiritual Awakening', S1 E1 2020. The Speaker is Mitchell Gibson. The Message Company presents The International Conference on Science & Consciousness.
159   Newton, Michael, *Journey of Souls* (p. 102). Llewellyn Worldwide, LTD. Kindle Edition.
160   Who Is Archangel Metatron? Keeper of the Book of Life. (n.d.). *Ask-Angels.Com.* Retrieved December 26, 2022, from https://www.ask-angels.com/channeled-messages/archangel-metatron/

down above the other. These two interconnecting pyramids in Metatron's Cube are the Merkaba ascension vehicle.

The Merkaba energy is believed, by many, to be a method of transporting entities from the Earthly plane into the heavens to be with God. According to some, Metatron's cube holds the script of Creation, the secrets of the universe, and the template for reality.[161] It can be used as a vehicle to travel to higher dimensions and maintain balanced energies in your body.

The three syllables making up the word Merkaba (Merkabah) translate to light, spirit, and body.[162] It is your spirit or light body that can transcend this world into the metaphysical realm.[163]

I was guided by a great bird spirit of translucent, divine light in my QHHT session vision. Was the great, white bird spirit created from Merkaba energy? The word 'Ba', in ancient Egypt, was a hawk with a human head. It was the Egyptians' way of depicting how the soul could freely float away from its physical body after death.[164]

---

161   Crawford, H. (2019, December 15). 9 Compelling Signs You Are Being Guided By Archangel Metatron. *Numerologist. Com*. https://numerologist.com/spiritual-growth/spiritual-world/9-signs-guided-by-archangel-metatron/
162   Merkaba Meditation: What Is The Merkaba And How To Activate It! (2019, July 4). *Relax Like A Boss*. https://relaxlikeaboss.com/merkaba-meditation/
163   Consciousreminder. (2019, September 5). Understanding The Merkaba, Your Inter-Dimensional Light Body. *Conscious Reminder*. https://consciousreminder.com/2019/09/05/understanding-the-merkaba-your-inter-dimensional-light-body/
164   *Ba | Egyptian religion | Britannica*. (n.d.). Retrieved December 21, 2022, from https://www.britannica.com/topic/ba-Egyptian-religion

The embossed, gold embroidery I saw on the empty throne at the beginning of my QHHT visions were most likely many Metatron's Cubes with the Merkaba in the middle of each cube. I think I just missed my Merkaba vehicle ride in my QHHT vision. It took a lot of energy to madly try and keep up with the great, white, bird spirit guiding me toward the gates of heaven (described in the Tape 1 section of Chapter 6). My feet were starting to get cold chasing this vision and Alannah had to put extra blankets on them.

Was Archangel Metatron showing me the way he ascended into heaven without dying? Merkaba comes from the Hebrew word for a chariot of light.[165]

When reading The Reluctant Messenger-Tales from Beyond Belief: An ordinary person's extraordinary journey into the unknown, I was excited to learn that the author, Candice Sanderson, had gone through the same learning curve I am experiencing. Her strange dreams and visions, as described in her book, were amazing and very powerful. These visions show a reality beyond our physical bodies. It is the greater reality of our souls and our Higher Selves. The visions are showing the reality of God.

I was able to correspond with Candice. I wanted her to know that some of the visions she described in her books were very similar to what I was experiencing. She had even created a multi-year journal of all her strange visions and dreams like

---

165   Dzierżawa, A. (2020, August 6). *What is a merkabah?* A Journey to Yourself | Duchowość | Spirituality. https://www.ajourneytoyourself.com/merkabah/

my *Religion of One* blog site (relofone.blogspot.com). There were several visions of pyramids during my QHHT session. The pyramids in my QHHT session visions were used for my protection, transfer of higher vibrational energy into lower vibrational souls, and transport of new/old souls to and from Earth. Candice Sanderson came to similar conclusions based on the following excerpt from her book, The Reluctant Messenger.

The following passage from Candice's book matches my visions of the root poking at my belly button, my birthing location, in deep space. She has the same keywords I had in my vision but interpreted the meaning with a greater depth of metaphysical knowledge and experience than I have. The excerpt from her book even matches my visions of ascended masters, one of the tall wise men I saw with a golden staff at the gates of heaven, and my vision of Mary holding the Christ Child…

… I attended a group angel meditation about a month later at the same church. As soon as the meditation began, I saw myself encased in the center of a spinning, three-dimensional shape formed by two pyramids, one pointing up and one facing down.

One pyramid spun clockwise, the other counterclockwise. As I floated in this timeless space, the messages began:

June 7, 2016

It is a birthing. This foundation born upon you is a new body, a body of light. It is charged by vibrations of the utmost high. There is nothing it cannot do. There is nothing you cannot do, for you are empowered with divine light. I bestow upon you the light of the ages, the light that led the wise men to the Christ Child. For this is the light of the divine, the light of wisdom, the light of truth. It is the lighted path of the Buddha, our most beloved Enlightened One. It is the lighted path upon which all ascended masters have trod. We give to you this roadmap. It is yours. It is within you and always has been. We have only lit the path for you to see. You must take the first step upon this path of wisdom. We are with you, and we shall remain by your side as you traverse this path for which you are destined.

I later learned that this double-pyramid shape was called a Merkaba, also known as a star tetrahedron. It was described as a divine vehicle of light used by ascended masters to connect with higher realms.[166] *It matched the message's description of a new body empowered with divine light. Once again, my after-the-fact research confirmed the information I had received. Guidance is within, like an internal GPS lighting your path. But it is only a guidepost, a suggestion. Would I be able to hear the subtle messages, leading me gently down this path of truth and wisdom? Would I be able to step on this divine path and follow it? I hoped so.*[167] [168]

166   Merkabah, Ezekiel's Wheel—Crystalinks. (n.d.). Retrieved December 26, 2022, from http://crystalinks.com/merkaba.html
167   Sanderson, Candice. The Reluctant Messenger-Tales from Beyond Belief: An ordinary person's extraordinary journey into the unknown (p. 265). Clark Press. Kindle Edition.
168   Ibid, (p. 214-215)

The Power of Crystals and Higher Vibrational Frequencies

The tetrahedron is a three-dimensional, four-sided pyramid geometric shape. Quartz and diamonds have a tetrahedral molecular structure. Crystalline-shaped pyramids were prevalent in my QHHT session visions. There were also several visions of intense light coming in and going out of crystalline pyramids.

When people started getting less sick from Covid-19, I ventured a quick trip to Palm Springs on an airplane in the dead of winter to escape the persistent rain in the Pacific Northwest and get my body out of the self-induced Covid-19 prison I had placed myself in for almost two years. I flew to Palm Springs by myself and some friends from the San Diego area drove up and stayed a couple of nights to visit with me.

I decided to visit a crystal shop specializing in merchandise made for different astrological, healing, and meditation purposes. The crystal shop was located in the funky, old, downtown area of Palm Springs. I wanted to purchase a few crystal-shaped objects for the first time in my life. It was an action on my part to seal the fact I was deep into the metaphysical realm and could use a little support when I needed it.

Visiting the crystal shop was my first step into the commercial world of psychics and astrologists. I have to say it felt like I was walking into a shop on Diagon Alley where

Harry Potter[169] bought all his school supplies. The people I saw shopping kept to themselves and gave me quick, suspicious glances. I suppressed the uneasy feelings I was getting and started browsing the merchandise. There was a locked glass case displayed on one of the side walls of the store with what I assumed to be more valuable, higher-quality crystal objects. One clear, oblong, tetrahedral-shaped (pyramid-shaped) crystal about a quarter inch in diameter was vibrating like a Sonicare toothbrush. Everyone else in the shop did not seem to be alarmed. I found it quite disturbing. It was the only thing vibrating with such intensity in the whole shop and there was no visible force making the crystal vibrate in the glass enclosure. It started to freak me out a little so I quickly walked past it and looked for less intense crystal objects I could purchase. After a few minutes, I went back to the glass case to see if the single, clear crystal was still vibrating.

Yes, it was!

I sometimes wonder if this was a sign for me to buy the vibrating crystal. Then I remember all the scary, ghostly TV series I have watched, in the past, with dire warnings given about picking up possessed objects and ending up also bringing home evil spirits attached to the objects that wreak havoc on your mind and your physical home life.

The cashiers at the crystal shop were quite happy. There seemed to be a steady stream of traffic into their shop buying different things. The suspicious glares and vibrating crystal

169   Harry Potter. (2022). In Wikipedia. _https://en.wikipedia.org/w/index.php?title=Harry_Potter&oldid=1127479423_

made this a memorable moment for me. It was a taste of Diagon Alley in Palm Springs.

Since the Palm Springs crystal shop experience, I have learned the fiercely vibrating crystal could have been confirmation from Archangel Metatron he was with me as I committed to delving a little further into the spiritual and metaphysical realm.

Archangel Metatron is known as the Angel of Ascension.[170] The Sonicare level of intense vibrational energy coming from the single crystal displayed in the Palm Springs crystal shop was of the same intensity that others have reported when dealing with Archangel Metatron. When Archangel Metatron is present to assist you in moving toward ascension to a higher vibrational level of consciousness, he can be extremely intense. The intense light of the Archangel is brought forth to help you with ascension and help you heal your body and soul.[171] I had visions of the powerful, healing, angelic light used during the Reiki healing portion of my QHHT session with Alannah. The healing light was so bright and powerful that I could not see how the angels were applying the light to my body to heal it.[172]

It has taken almost two years of research on metaphysical concepts to get to the point where I understood what all the intense visions Metatron chose to show me meant in

170   Hall, B. (2022, June 24). Archangel Metatron: Angel of Ascension and Spiritual Transformation. *Paranormal Authority*. https://paranormalauthority.com/archangel-metatron/
171   Crawford, H. (2019, December 15). 9 Compelling Signs You Are Being Guided By Archangel Metatron. *Numerologist. Com*. https://numerologist.com/spiritual-growth/spiritual-world/9-signs-guided-by-archangel-metatron/
172   Ibid.

my QHHT session with Alannah.

THE PERSISTENT SIKH CONNECTION

Why do I keep experiencing dreams, visions, and voices in my head about different religions and philosophies? Are they all related to each other somehow? I have read profound words from Buddha's teachings and powerful visions of Jesus. I experienced a Sikh guru performing a beautiful marriage ceremony for my nephew and his Sikh bride. Historically, the ten first leaders of the Sikh religion are defined as gurus.

Sikh comes from a Sanskrit root word for disciple or learner.[173]

Sikhs believe that…

Realization of Truth is higher than all else. Higher still is truthful living.

Sikh teaching emphasizes the principle of equality of all humans and rejects discrimination [based on] caste, creed…, and gender.[174]

Sikhs believe in one god and stress the equality of all men and women. They emphasize service to humanity. This is a very honorable and deserving foundation for humanity

---

173   'Sikhism and Islam: The Inter-Relationship', *Research Gate*, https://www.researchgate.net/publication/348975873_Sikhism_and_Islam_The_Inter-Relationship
174   'What does Sikh mean?', *Definitions*, https://www.defini-tions.net/definition/Sikh

to build upon anywhere.[175]

I heard a voice in my head, one day, say a word that is used in the native language of the Sikhs.

04-25-2022 A Voice in My Head Responded To A Thought I Had

I feel like I am more in tune with listening to fleeting voices in my head and paying close attention to strange dreams I have.

When I get a voice in my head responding immediately to the last thought I just had, it still feels a little unnerving, though.

On the afternoon of 04-25-2022, I closed my eyes to take a little nap. I had just placed a notebook on the nightstand and closed my eyes thinking,

'I don't know why I placed a notebook beside my bed just now.'

I got an immediate response. The response was quick so I could only clearly remember the last half of the statement – in fact, I wrote it down before trying to take my quick nap.

'Ji saves the world.'

I was sure of the spelling of Ji when I wrote the message. … I have never heard of the word Ji before. What does this

175   Who are Sikhs? What is Sikhism? (2012, August 5). SikhNet. http://www.sikhnet.com/pages/who-are-sikhs-what-is-sikhism

mean? Who is this person?[176]

I learned that *Ji* is used in Punjabi. Punjabi is the language of Sikhs and other South Asian cultures. It is a term that provides a way of showing respect for the person or object mentioned.

-ji ... is a gender-neutral honorific used as a suffix in many languages of the Indian subcontinent, such as Hindi and Punjabi languages and their dialects prevalent in northern India, north-west and central India.

Ji is gender-neutral and can be used as a term of respect for [a] person, relationships, or inanimate objects as well. Its usage is similar, but not identical, to another Subcontinental honorific, sāhab. It is similar to the gender-neutral Japanese honorific san.[177]

Guru Nanak Dev Ji founded the Sikh religion in the fifteenth century in Northern India.

The Difference Between Sikhism and Christianity

1. *Sikhism is based on the teachings of the ten gurus contained in Guru Granth Sahib while Christianity is based on the life and teachings of Jesus Christ.*

2. *Christianity is the largest religion in the world, with*

---

176   Major, M. 'A Voice In My Head Responded To A Thought I Had,' *Religion of One* (04-25-2022). https://relofone.blogspot.com/2022/04/04-25-2022-voice-in-my-head-responded.html
177   -Ji. (2022). In *Wikipedia*. https://en.wikipedia.org/w/index.php?title=-ji&oldid=1094382195

Sikhism being the fifth.

3. *Sikhs regard their god to be shapeless, timeless, and sightless while Christians regard Jesus as the Supreme God.*[178]

Opinions regarding the differences between Sikhism and Christianity vary from the above list. Other people may argue Jesus is the Son of God but not God himself, for example.[179]

Sikhism has many beliefs matching my QHHT visions and the responsibilities of Metatron.

Sikhism believes in predestination within God's will, and what one does, speaks, and hears falls within that will; one has to simply follow the laid down path (per God's hukam).[180]

I was told to keep on the path when I was walking along a path of crystals as mentioned in this book's Chapter 6, Tape 3 QHHT session section.

I found it very odd that historical facts about the Sikh religion kept popping up when researching possible reasons for the strange metaphysical dreams, visions, and voices I have heard in my head. One common thread between Buddha, Jesus, and the Sikhs is their dedication to teaching us the ultimate spiritual

178   *Difference Between Sikhism And Christianity | Difference Between.* (n.d.). Retrieved December 21, 2022, from http://www.differencebetween.net/miscellaneous/difference-between-sikhism-and-christianity/?msclkid=d6bae475c7d711ec-96d76223a71dced4
179   'Jesus', *Lexico*, https://www.lexico.com/en/definition/jesus
180   Hukam. (2021). In *Wikipedia*. https://en.wikipedia.org/w/index.php?title=Hukam&oldid=1046972121

meaning of reality. They all explain the steps you need to take to become spiritually enlightened to the greater meaning of your reality.[181]

I now believe my spirit guides are making me aware of the common thread transcending all the major religions of love, peace, and harmony; and gurus and other great teachers are showing us the way.

I had a dream that revealed we have entered an age (of Aquarius) where the power is turning over to the individual. Each person now has the freedom to choose their reality based on what aligns with their soul...

On 01-24-2022, I had a dream where a voice in my head announced, 'This is the year of the Sokuba'. I had never heard that word before, but I found a translation for its meaning: This is the year of being or the year to be me.

The Zulu translation of *isimo sokuba khona* is *the state of being.*

When I started my *Religion of One* blog in 2005[182] I defined the greatest level of mankind as being One with God.

In the beginning, there was just one mass and one force. The One Force was God. After the Big Bang, the definition

---

181   'Initiation or Empowerment: what is it, why it is important in Vajrayana, how it helps, when you need it, how to receive it', *Buddha Weekly: Buddhist Practices, Mindfulness, Meditation,* https://buddhaweekly.com/initiation-empowerment-important-vajraya-na-helps-need-receive/
182   Major, M. 'Fate,' *Religion of One* (10-19-2005). https://relo-fone.blogspot.com/2005/10/fate.html

of mass became random and comes in many more forms. More forms of mass than we have yet to even imagine. Perhaps consciousness or need is simply a type of mass all living things have control over to generate the 'hunt and gather' instinct. This need generates the powerful instinct to survive. I have previously described this instinct as the desire to get back to being one again with God. We all have an innate need for God ... to become One again with God.

I believe there are bonds at the quantum level we do not understand yet. These bonds may make up a mass of paranormal resources we need to survive. Living things already know how to tap into and use the forces available at the quantum physics level of existence. Bonds between random waves may be a way of stabilizing what would otherwise be a completely random world.[183]

Ancient Link Languages

I found out there have been specific link languages developed for various reasons in history. There are languages used specifically to communicate across cultures for trade transactions and recording religious doctrines.

Sanskrit is the sacred language of Hinduism, the language of classical Hindu philosophy, and of historical texts of Buddhism and Jainism. It was a link language in ancient and medieval South Asia, and upon transmission of Hindu and Buddhist culture to Southeast Asia, East Asia,

183   Ibid.

*and Central Asia in the early medieval era, it became a
language of religion and high culture ...* [184]

Link languages were used to bridge the communication of
religious beliefs and trade across various cultures within the
Indo-Aryan region. The Indo-Aryan region is mainly found
in the northern regions of India and surrounding countries.[185]
The merging of Europeans into the mainly Indian Aryan region
created a branch of Indo-European languages. It is said Jesus
spoke Aramaic most of the time.

*Aramaic was used by the common people, while Hebrew
remained the language of religion and government and of
the upper class.*[186]

The physical regions on Earth where all the religions and
philosophies I have dreamt about originated from a common
area where there were well-established trade routes. Northern
India and the Mideast countries of Turkey, Israel, Syria, Iraq,
Iran, and Egypt were well-traveled by many religious and
philosophical leaders such as Pythagoras. It has been said,

*Buddhist missionaries were sent by Emperor Ashoka of
India to Syria, Egypt, and Greece beginning in 250 BC*

184   Sanskrit. (2022). In *Wikipedia*. https://en.wikipedia.org/w/
index.php?title=Sanskrit&oldid=1128447769
185   Indo-Aryan peoples. (2022). In *Wikipedia*. https://
en.wikipedia.org/w/index.php?title=Indo-Aryan_peoples&ol-
did=1128911762
186   *Aramaic language | Description, History, & Facts | Britannica*.
(n.d.). Retrieved December 21, 2022, from https://www.britannica.
com/topic/Aramaic-language

and may have helped prepare for the ethics of Christ.[187]

How could the Buddhist missionaries explain their Buddhist beliefs to people who only spoke Aramaic or Hebrew in the countries they were sent to?

Sanskrit was the native language of Buddhists and also a link language many people could speak along the established trade routes between northern India and the Mideast countries where the Buddhist missionaries were sent.

The Nazi regime, during World War II, warped the Aryan race into a master race of Nordic or Germanic descent, which may have been based on the following information.

...the original speakers of the Indo-European languages and their descendants up to the present day constitute a distinctive race or subrace of the larger Caucasian race. Aryanism developed as a racial ideology that claimed that the Aryan race was a master race. While originally meant simply as a neutral ethno-linguistic classification, from the late 19th century onwards the concept of the Aryan race has been used by proponents of ideologically-motivated racism and white supremacism such as in doctrines of Nazism and neo-Nazism.[188]

The fact I had a QHHT vision of Jesus and about thirteen

187   Buddhism and Christianity. (2022). In *Wikipedia*. https://en.wikipedia.org/w/index.php?title=Buddhism_and_Christianity&oldid=1121370575
188   '*What does aryan mean?* (n.d.). Retrieved December 26, 2022, from https://www.definitions.net/definition/aryan

tall, blond, Nordic-looking entities in white flowing robes is disturbing to me. The tall, blond, Nordic-looking entities fit the Nazi profile of the Aryan Master race they made up. I was not the one who warped these types of entities into non-Jewish, pro-Nazi, supreme beings.

I found out my ancestors, on my mom's side, came from an area of France with a high density of descendants from Scandinavian countries. This shows up in my Ancestry.com DNA results. Some of my extended family members have had various shades of blond to reddish-blond hair and blue eyes during their toddler years and afterward. I never had blond hair. I have always had dark brunette hair from my father's Italian lineage.

There are references to a tall white or blond-haired race considered to be the Watchers in the Book of Enoch and also interpreted to be the Fallen Angels by some.[189]

Jesus did not have Aryan features in my QHHT vision. He was pictured with auburn hair. Auburn hair is between the tall, pure Aryan blond hair and the dark (brunette) hair humans had in my vision.

---

189   *Could the Annunaki be the watchers mentioned in the Bible?* (n.d.). Quora. Retrieved December 21, 2022, from https://www.quora.com/Could-the-Annunaki-be-the-watchers-mentioned-in-the-Bible.

ASTROLOGICAL AND NUMEROLOGICAL REFERENCES TO ARCHANGEL METATRON

Each of the twelve zodiac signs has a specific archangel assigned to them. Archangel Metatron is associated with the zodiac sign of Virgo (August 23–September 22). Archangel Jophiel is associated with the zodiac sign of Libra (September 23–October 22).[190] Eric Lucas said he could provide a more accurate description of my personality and traits if I told him the specific day and time I was born. We never returned to this subject before he passed away.

Because Archangel Metatron uses the Metatron's Cube as a powerful, source of energy to heal our bodies and clear away burdensome lower energies within our chakras, he has been associated with the astrological sign of Virgo. Virgo is strongly associated with healing (conventional or alternative) and service to others.[191] The Virgin Mary has also been associated with the Virgo sign.[192]

My sign is Libra (born between September 23 and October 22) which is right next to Virgo (born between August 23 and

190   13 Archangels (Essences) of Creation. (n.d.). Https://Www. Universallifetools.Com/. Retrieved December 21, 2022, from *https:// www.universallifetools.com/2013/09/article-8-the-13-archangels/*
191   whoismyguardianangel. (n.d.). VIRGO AND ARCHANGEL METATRON [Tumblr]. *Tumblr.* Retrieved December 26, 2022, from https://whoismyguardianangel.tumblr.com/post/148402259110/ virgo-and-archangel-metatron
192   'Virgo - The Virgin - Astrology - The White Goddess', http://www.thewhitegoddess.co.uk/divination/astrology/vir-go_-_the_virgin.asp

September 22) in astrology.[193] I discovered many new revelations about Metatron at the start of Virgo's astrological calendar period for 2022. Is it a coincidence I have found fresh insight into the astrological relationships of the amazing visions I had in the past and how they relate to Metatron during the Virgo calendar period of 2022?

Lisa Mendes is an editor of my book and an astrologer. Her website for astrology is Astrologysphere.com. When Lisa reviewed this chapter of my book she suggested I get my astrology chart done by an astrologist. My sun, in astrology, is Libra. According to Lisa, my moon may be in Virgo. I have to find out the exact time I was born to verify what sign my moon is in. Having a moon in Virgo could be interpreted as further evidence my soul is a member of Metatron's soul family.

In Hebrew numerology, the consonants in the name Metatron have preassigned numeric values. Shaddai is the Hebrew word for Almighty. God is considered the Almighty in ancient Hebrew literature. Each consonant in the name Shaddai has a preassigned Hebrew numerology number, as well. If you add the preassigned numeric values of each consonant in the name Metatron and compare the total to the sum of all the numeric values for the consonants in the Hebrew name Shaddai you will find both names add up, numerically, to 314. The conclusion from having the same core Hebrew number, found in an ancient Hebrew text, is that Metatron acts as the voice of God to humankind. Metatron communicates with God directly

---

193   'What Are the 12 Zodiac Sign Dates?', *Astrology.com*, https://www.astrology.com/article/zodiac-sign-dates/

and is the mediator between God and humankind.

I had visions of the sacred geometry used in Metatron's cube because these were visions Metatron wanted me to try and understand. Lotus petal-shaped transportation pods were used to transport newly created souls into our three-dimensional (3-D) universe from the heavenly realm in one of my QHHT session visions (Ref. Chapter 3, *Tape 3*). The lotus petal shape is revealed at the overlapping intersections of the thirteen circles making up Metatron's Cube.

When I read excerpts discussing *Metatron's Cube vs. The Lotus Of Eternal Life And Is 666 Evil?* — *Rahan Spirituality*, I noticed many keywords matching my otherworldly dreams and visions. The reference to a lotus throne being a mode of transportation linked to the Merkaba (found within Metatron's Cube) is truly remarkable. It matches my very strange QHHT session vision of lotus petal-shaped transportation pods used to transport brand-new souls to destinations in our 3-D universe.

> *...When we experience enough lives to gain the knowledge of who we are once again, we simply graduate from the third dimension or more specifically Earth school and into a new paradigm of a higher reality beyond time and space. When enough squares have been played through your various Earthly incarnations and you've been on the other side of the coin for every situation, you begin to see the whole picture of creation. ... Once you fill in all the gaps with your spiritual knowledge which only comes down to one core principle, to love in every situation, will your*

vibration pass beyond that of matter.

This is where the Lotus of eternal life comes in and is the transition into becoming a crystalline being. Have you ever wondered why crystals are called what they are? The name broken-down is fragments of cryst, of Christ. The Lotus flower is a depiction of Christ Consciousness. This doesn't confine a being to a religious practice but that of divine existence. We see the Lotus throne depicted as the same as the Egyptians' ark of the million years or the ship of eternity which is referring to the ascension vehicle of the heart through the Merkaba. Metatron's Cube is the spiritual blueprint which gives us the wisdom to ascend to the higher realms where we connect directly to Source energy[194]

I don't think I have played all the squares in the circle of creation yet. I have been told, more than once, that I may be still missing a few squares... I get the feeling Metatron thinks I am slow at figuring out things and that I need lots of nudges to keep me on the right path to gain the knowledge required to achieve spiritual enlightenment in this lifetime. The hint I received today came in the revelation I was starting to notice a combination of two numbers, 11:13. After looking on the internet I found out it means I should start solving my problems one at a time and not get frustrated with my slow but steady efforts. It is also confirmation my spirit guides are supporting

194   Awakening Your Soul | Metatron's Cube vs The Lotus of Eternal Life and is 666 really evil. (n.d.). Retrieved December 26, 2022, from *https://www.facebook.com/groups/Awakeningyoursoul.1111/posts/1626069370909839/*

me in my efforts to get things done.[195]

Lesson learned? I am almost finished drafting this book, so take it to the end with the confidence your spirit guides will help you complete it.

One internet source has taken the analysis of Metatron's Cube into an abstract mathematical model, in the fifth dimension, with functioning torus fields and spacetime continuum grids—all originating from the eighth dimension and beyond.[196] I am not afraid to admit that this type of analysis is way beyond my level of comprehension. Interestingly, many of the keywords found in the article are mentioned in various parts of this book. I found the mathematical model discourse on ascension article on 11-29-2022… a lot of elevens can be derived from that date.

The Numbers 11 and 22

Metatron is well-known to present multiple elevens (11:11) in various formats to get your attention. Many people around the world have commented on the powerful messages they receive around the time they often start seeing multiple number elevens.

---

195   *11:13 – Meaning*. (n.d.). Retrieved December 21, 2022, from https://mydreamsymbolism.com/1113-meaning/.
196   The Lotus / Flower of Life, Krystic / Fibonacci Spiral & Metatron's Cube | The Evolutionary Ascension Discourse From The Gold Order Melchizedek Collective. (2021, February 28). https://evolutionaryascension.com/articles/the-lotus-of-life-the-flower-of-life/

I found the referenced article by Silverla St Michael[197] to be very enlightening. Her description of the spiritual meaning of seeing multiple elevens matches my experience of being awakened to the metaphysical side of my existence.

It was a relief to find out that noticing repeating number elevens was a positive sign of awakening to my spiritual self. The spiritual meaning of numbers in numerology, astrology, and the metaphysical realm is well documented.

If I can generate the number 11 by adding each digit of significant dates, using the numbers in mm/dd/yy or mm/dd/yyyy format, I believe, it is confirmation from Metatron that the event is definitely significant or is directly related to an action generated by Metatron. Seeing the same number everywhere also opens the door to the idea there are other significant formulas for generating specific sequences of numbers that may help humanity understand the true scope of metaphysical resources available to them in this world and beyond.

Broadening our perspective of reality to encompass the spiritual realm and using new formulas to help explain the spiritual realm could be a very positive advancement for the whole human race ... physically, mentally, and spiritually.

Spirit guides are ready and waiting to help us understand a greater reality than we currently know. Silverla St Michael states Metatron can show up in unexpected situations as he did in my practice and pre-QHHT vision sessions when I did

197   *Archangel Directory – Mystical Mind, Angelic Heart.* (n.d.). Retrieved December 28, 2022, from https://mysticalmindangelicheart. wordpress.com/all-about-archangels/archangel-directory/

not even know who he was. She also states you know it is Metatron's calling card when you receive answers or statements in your head when you least suspect it.[198] Multiple elevens can be rendered by adding all the single digits together from the date I began my metaphysical journey (09-27-2020). This is an incredibly powerful validation that the voice in my head was Archangel Metatron's speaking directly to me, on 09-27-2020, since elevens are known to be his calling card.

Simone Mathews states,

[The word Angels in numerology ...] *resonates with Number 22 (11+11) ... it is a reminder that you are surrounded by Angels in that moment (& every moment) ... you are NEVER alone!*[199]

My mom's birthday was 12-22-22. Since twenty-two is such a powerful Angel Number made up of multiple elevens, it would make sense my mother had a soul family connection with Archangel Metatron, as well...and her spirit still does.

In one of my first QHHT session visions, I slowly moved past a vision of Mother Mary nurturing a baby in her arms. Metatron has the responsibility for nurturing sensitive children. He helps them use their sensitivities without fear, like psychic powers, for the good of humanity. With each generation, Metatron is

198   'Archangel Metatron', *Mystical Mind*, https://mysticalmin-dangelicheart.wordpress.com/all-about-archangels/archangel-me-tatron/.

199   13 Archangels (Essences) of Creation. (n.d.). *Https://Www. Universallifetools.Com/*. Retrieved December 28, 2022, from https://www.universallifetools.com/2013/09/article-8-the-13-archangels/

showing me the weaving fabric of love nurtured within each of our soul family connections from one generation to another. This eternal fabric of love bursts out and reveals itself in full color after you are spiritually awakened.

Archangel Metatron is responsible for safeguarding the Tree of Life which is also represented in Metatron's Cube.[200] The Tree of Life represents our relationship with our ancestors. I established my *relofone.blogspot.com* blog site based on the idea that there are many branching patterns, like trees and rivers. The many branches of each of our family trees consist of the historical families we are connected with at birth. There is a whole other tree within us that reflects our spiritual soul and its connection with our unique soul family.[201] There is a weave of loving, eternal soul family connections that can be used when we need protection from the harsh, cold realities of life.

Archangel Michael

After my traumatic ordeal with fleshy roots and aliens with see-through heads, my QHHT vision was of Archangel Metatron relaxing in a recliner. Metatron showed me where he goes to rest. It was a nice condo on the top floor of a Spanish-style building…in heaven? A beautiful, dark blue angel was hovering slightly above and behind him where a condo wall should have been. Alannah told me she witnessed this blue aura fill the QHHT session room

200   Who Are the Angels on the Kabbalah Tree of Life? (n.d.). Learn Religions. Retrieved December 28, 2022, from https://www. learnreligions.com/angels-kabbalah-tree-of-life-124294
201   What Does the Tree of Life Mean? - SoulPulse. (2022, September 28). https://soulpulse.org/what-does-the-tree-of-life-mean/

during my vision while the other lights in the room went dim. Who was this blue angel hovering over my vision of Archangel Metatron and, at the same time, filling my QHHT session room with a soft, blue aura?

My QHHT session vision of an angel bathed in blue hovering behind Archangel Metatron was most likely Archangel Michael. Descriptions of Archangel Michael acknowledge he often has a powerful blue or purplish-blue aura of light surrounding him.[202,203]

Archangel Michael is known as the guardian and is in charge of all angels. He is also known to be someone you can call to protect you when you need it. This is why he showed up in my vision right after I had a traumatic experience with strange things I thought were attacking me in the deepest, darkest part of our cosmos.

The Thirteen Elements of Creation

In my final QHHT session vision, I saw thirteen tall beings in heaven near Jesus. They were all floating on white, billowy clouds just like in the stained-glass First Vision depiction of God, Jesus, and Joseph Smith.[204] This was a powerful vision, and I did not understand its meaning at the time it occurred.

202   Archangel Michael. (2017, October 20). Angel Numbers | Zodiac | Astrology | Tarot. https://thesecretofthetarot.com/arch-angel-michael/.
203   Archangel Michael | Angel Messenger RE. (n.d.). Retrieved December 28, 2022, from https://www.angelmessenger.net/arch-angel-michael/
204   First Vision. (2022). In *Wikipedia*. https://en.wikipedia.org/w/index.php?title=First_Vision&oldid=1125354842

I discovered that there are thirteen elements of creation in our universe. There are thirteen spheres in Metatron's cube representing these divine elements of creation. Jesus and the thirteen tall beings were Archangel Metatron's way of showing me the wondrous things in our universe, including humans, that he helped create.

The Number 13 [and Metatron's Cube]

... it has 13 spheres. With all of them held together by several lines drawn through the midpoint of the central circle to connect with every other circle in the Metatron's Cube. The straight lines' name is Masculine, while the spheres or circles' name is Feminine.

Consequently, it depicts the weaving together of male and female polarities in creating the ONENESS field of the infinite ALL.

The 13 circles stand for 13 archangels, who stand before God. Each of them keeps an element of creation.[205]

Could the above quote be the explanation for the last vision of my QHHT session of Jesus, thirteen tall beings, and the human couple in a wedding dress and tuxedo overlooking the infinite universe— the infinite ALL? Perhaps my vision was shown to me by Archangel Metatron so I could realize that we were created in the eye of God as a part of Earth as well as a part of the grand plan for the entire universe. My blog site was named *The*

205   The Metatron's Cube Meaning Explained — Sacred Geometry. (2018, May 1). *The Mystica.* https://www.themystica.com/meta-trons-cube/

Religion of One in 2005. The name for my blog site was probably an idea planted in my head by Metatron in 2005. He wanted to make sure I understood, *We are one with the universe.*

According to what I have seen from the James Webb telescope images shared with the public at webbtelescope.org,

We are not the only ones in the universe.

How will humanity handle this revelation if it is true?

My previous visions of enlightenment, from Archangel Metatron suggested the idea that alien civilizations must follow the same path to spiritual enlightenment we are being asked to follow. I even had one dream where there were a couple of aliens on my afterlife review committee telling me I took the easy way out in my last life on Earth.[206]

ARCHANGEL METATRON AND INDIGO/CRYSTAL CHILDREN

Of all the responsibilities of Archangel Metatron explained in existing literature the one that shocked me the most was the idea of Archangel Metatron specifically watching over Indigo, Crystal, and Star children. What are Indigo, Crystal, and Star children? I am going to concentrate on the definition of Indigo children because it matches the experience in my life the best.

---

206   Major, M. 'I Took the Easy Way Out!', *Religion of One* (05-15-2018). https://relofone.blogspot.com/2018/05/05-15-2018-i-took-easy-way-out.html

Definition of Indigo

A tropical plant of the pea family, which was formerly widely cultivated as a source of dark blue dye.

The dark blue dye obtained from the indigo plant.

A color between blue and violet in the spectrum: The deepest indigo of the horizon.[207]

My most familiar use of the word 'indigo' defines its unique dark blue color. Indigo children do not have dark blue skin but their aura is known to be the unique color of indigo.[208]

Archangel Metatron is said to watch over Indigo souls and sensitive children, in general. He helps channel their sensitivities toward positive achievements with confidence to guide all of us in the evolution of our souls. Archangel Metatron, according to information published on the internet, has a special interest in helping people on Earth with Attention Deficit Hyperactivity Disorder (ADHD).[209]

Because of my Attention Deficit Disorder (ADD), I take a fairly strong dosage of the generic brand of Concerta so I do not get too distracted anymore by something else I find more interesting. The generic brand of Concerta helps me concentrate on a single task and see it through to completion.

---

207   Powered by Oxford Languages
208   'Indigo Aura Color' | *Indigo Test For Children & Adults*. (n.d.). Retrieved December 25, 2022, from http://www.indigotest.org/tag/indigo-aura-color/
209   shellster1. (2014, February 21). *Archangel Metatron*. https://myspiritualoasis.com/2014/02/21/archangel-metatron/

I have performed better in this reincarnation on Earth than in previous ones. On the ADD medicine, I also learned I have some talent for illustrating/painting people and scenes on canvas and watercolor paper.

Indigo children's purpose is to eradicate antiquated structures and systems weighing down the evolution of all souls on Earth. They are here on Earth to introduce a new, higher vibrational level of existence of love and compassion to our world. They are highly sensitive and have a strong bond with the spiritual realm where they can tap into intense, positive energy sources to guide the world to a better understanding of the spiritual evolution requirements of their souls.[210]

> *They enter this life often overwhelmed and confused by the negativity and heavy energy that permeates, which can cause them severe problems — emotionally, physically, mentally, socially, and energetically... He [Metatron] works with these children to provide them with the tools and skills of empowerment and fearless courage to fulfill their purposes.*[211]

Maybe that is why I cried so hard as a baby that I turned blue in the face. I was highly sensitive and overwhelmed with the Earthly environment I was newly born into.

Indigo children are known to have the following additional

210   Brown, S. (2019, May 17). Who is Archangel Metatron? And What is The Metatron Cube? The Black Feather Intuitive. *https://www.theblackfeatherintuitive.com/archangel-metatron/*
211   Ibid.

personality traits:

- *Are empathic, curious, and strong-willed*

- *Are often perceived by friends and family as being strange*

- *Possess a clear sense of self-definition and purpose*

- *Show a strong innate subconscious spirituality from early childhood (which, however, does not necessarily imply a direct interest in spiritual or religious areas)*

- *Have a strong feeling of entitlement, or deserving to be here*

- *High intelligence quotient*

- *Inherent intuitive ability*

- *Resistance to rigid, control-based paradigms of authority.*[212]

There are many times I have been resistant to *rigid, control-based paradigms of authority* from a very young age when I became a Catholic school kindergarten dropout.

Another example of a situation where it would have been safer for me to back down was when I wrote a paper for a Fisheries Management class at the University of Washington. I challenged a teacher in college who was teaching the course. The course had something to do with all the different ways to create energy. We were given the assignment to write a paper explaining all the

---

212   *Archangel Metatron.* (2017, October 20). Angel Numbers | Zodiac | Astrology | Tarot. https://thesecretofthetarot.com/archangel-metatron/.

advantages of nuclear-powered energy sources.[213] After careful research, I concluded that the nuclear waste generated from nuclear power plants was radioactive, extremely harmful to humans, and had a half-life of twenty-thousand years or more, which could never be a good thing.

I had to go to my teacher's office and negotiate the failed grade he gave me on my paper to bring it up to a B grade. I was steadfast in explaining what I thought were the obvious facts I had carefully researched regarding how horrible the twenty-thousand-year half-life of radioactive material was, how mismanaged the disposal of radioactive waste from nuclear plants has been, and how nuclear energy waste would be a great burden for generations of humans after we both had died because they did not know how to safely dispose of it for thousands of years.

My teacher finally admitted he had been spewing out the same spiel for so many years, that he had forgotten to keep up with the current, damaging evidence being collected regarding the extremely radioactive nuclear energy sources in current use and the far-reaching implications regarding the mismanagement of nuclear waste material disposal. Even today, it is recommended by the Oregon and Washington Department of Fisheries to stop or limit the consumption of many different fish species caught in various areas of the Columbia River. This is due to toxic waste contamination of the fish caught in the Columbia

213   *U.S. nuclear industry – U.S. Energy Information Administration (EIA).* (n.d.). Retrieved December 29, 2022, from https://www.eia.gov/energyexplained/nuclear/us-nuclear-industry.php

River. These consumption limitations include fish caught in the Columbia River near the location of the Hanford nuclear waste storage site.[214] Billions of dollars more are predicted to be spent to try and clean up the Hanford waste site of all the leaking, buried radioactive waste material.[215] Right now, they have made decisions to leave some of this leaking waste alone. This is not a good solution, in my opinion.

The concept of Indigo children is not generally well-accepted. The definition and characteristics of Indigo children diagnosed with attention deficit hyperactivity disorder (ADHD) or Attention Deficit Disorder (minus hyperactivity; ADD) match my personality and actions in many ways. However, I am going to accept the idea that Indigo children are a real thing and I may be one myself.

I do not feel motivated to jump up on a pulpit and start preaching. I get overwhelmed with too many people and too much stimulus at once makes me freeze- my brain just shuts off. My blue-screen brain meltdown behavior was first discovered when I was designated to sing a solo at a parents' night for my first-grade class. Parents' night is when the parents attend a scheduled review with their first grader's teacher. The teacher's students attend, as well, and put on a show for the parents. The class shows highlights of all the things they have been working on and accomplished so far.

214   Contaminants in Fish. (n.d.). Washington State Department of Health. Retrieved December 21, 2022, from https://doh.wa.gov/community-and-environment/food/fish/contaminants-fish
215   'Billions could be saved in Hanford Site cleanup — Here's how. (n.d.). Energy Communities Alliance. Retrieved December 21, 2022, from http://www.energyca.org/eca-updates/2022/8/16/billions-could-be-saved-in-hanford-site-cleanup-heres-how

I remember feeling so confident and relaxed before the Parents' Night performance. However, when the time came to sing my solo portion from the song, *Waltzing Matilda*, I froze. I looked at all the parents staring back at me and I could not get out a single note. To this day I would never go to a bar and sing with a Karaoke machine. I seldom sing in public at all.

Even when you learn you have God-given talents, there may be very real Earthly, physical issues preventing you from sharing those talents with the world. Maybe Metatron was asked to be especially mindful of nurturing sensitive souls who get overwhelmed on the Earthly plane because he was from Earth and knows how hard it can be to accomplish tasks when you are overwhelmed with emotions and excess stimuli hitting your senses all at once. Dr. Elaine Aron has discovered 'over-stimulation' is quite common in Highly Sensitive People (HSP).[216]

Did my first-grade experience create a great trauma in my life I never got over? Some might say so. I never sang a solo in public again. Having ADD does have the advantage of not dwelling on past problems for very long. I am easily distracted by other things I become more interested in. I never seem to have time to dwell on the past. I believe it is important to concentrate on positive actions you know are achievable in your lifetime and share what you have learned with others. I am more productive by sharing what I have learned along the way in less, in-your-

---

216   Hill, M. (2015, November 16). The DOES Model Of Elaine Aron. Sensitive Evolution. https://sensitiveevolution.com/sensitive-evolution-library/does-model-elaine-aron/

face, public ways like blogging. I have learned to speak publicly through the massive number of presentations you are required to do when getting a Master of Business Administration in college. It is still not my favorite thing to do, and I avoid it.

MY MAGENTA PYRAMID CELL PHONE SCREENSAVER

The default screen display on the mobile phone I bought online four or five years ago came with this image of pyramid-shaped, magenta crystals. Three replacement phones later, I still have the pyramid-shaped, magenta crystals picture as the default on my current phone. I had no idea I would be able to relate this default phone screen to the ancient beginning of my eternal soul.

I found out I had a soul-family connection to Archangel Metatron right before I went into my QHHT session. Six months later, I started researching my pre-QHHT session recording and found out many artists depict Archangel Metatron dressed or bathed in a magenta color. I researched the meaning of the magenta color on the internet and found this definition:

Definition of Magenta

Magenta is uplifting to our spirits during times of unhappiness, anger, or frustration. In the meaning of colors, magenta represents universal love at its highest level. It promotes compassion, kindness, and cooperation and encourages a sense of self-respect and contentment in those who use it. A strong and inspiring color, magenta can appear outrageous and shocking on one hand, or innovative and imaginative on the other. It is creativity inspired by beauty.[217]

A quick check on the internet reveals Metatron has been known to be associated with the colors green, deep pink, indigo, and violet.[218, 219] The green and purple beads dream listed in Appendix 1 is one of my most puzzling, afterlife dreams. This dream may have been a hint I was related to Archangel Metatron. The dream was in 2014. It would be several years before I became

217   *The Color Magenta*. (n.d.). Empowered By Color. Retrieved December 26, 2022, from https://www.empower-yourself-with-color-psychology.com/color-magenta.html
218   *Angels & Colors: 7 Most Common Angel Light Colors Symbolism*. (n.d.). Amanda Linette Meder. Retrieved December 26, 2022, from https://www.amandalinettemeder.com/blog/angels-and-colors-meaning-and-symbolism-of-angelic-light-colors
219   *Meet Archangel Metatron, Angel of Life*. (n.d.). Learn Religions. Retrieved December 26, 2022, from https://www.learnreligions.com/meet-archangel-metatron-124083

aware of Metatron.[220]

I now believe the default cell phone screen with an image of magenta crystals represents the core of who I am and what I strive to be on a spiritual level. I am being lovingly guided in this life by Archangel Metatron and my soul family. The color magenta represents the unique vibrational frequency of my soul family.

Archangel Metatron can let himself be known to you using obnoxious, in-your-face signs like a repeating number eleven everywhere you look. He will repeat these signs or messages to you over and over again until you figure out what he is trying to tell you. He can also subtly voice his opinion in whispers as you are waking up or going to sleep.

The vast metaphysical research I have done to write this book has given me the peace of mind to recognize the signs early, so I do not go crazy seeing the same signs over and over again without having a clue who Archangel Metatron is and why he keeps bugging me.[221]

I can say I am now emotionally uplifted when I see his signs because I know his hints are positive reinforcement for the efforts I am currently engaged in. His persistent hints come from a source of pure love and compassion.

---

220   Major, M. 'Next Gadget Rage?, *Religion of One* (02-18-2014). https://relofone.blogspot.com/2014/02/02182014-next-gadget-rage.html
221   9 Compelling Signs You Are Being Guided By Archangel Metatron, *Numerologist.com,* https://numerologist.com/spiritu-al-growth/spiritual-world/9-signs-guided-by-archangel-metatron/

OTHER SPIRITUALLY ENLIGHTENING MOMENTS

On 08-18-2021, I had extensive back surgery to fuse my lower disks because I did not feel secure or stable. The disks were loose in my Root chakra area. They had popped out of alignment. The popped-out disks were randomly jabbing the raw nerves of my spinal cord, causing me extreme pain. I now have eight screws and a grid of horizontal and vertical metal rods to keep my lower back secure and stable.

I rented what turned out to be a very special house when I was in Phoenix for the back operation. As soon as I opened the door of the rental house for the first time, in front of me was a huge oil painting of a seated Buddha. The painting of Buddha made me feel calmer. The vibrations of the rental house with the giant Buddha painting exuded calming and healing energy.

My neurosurgeon's name was Dr. Krishna. I felt I was in good hands...

Krishna is a major deity in Hinduism. He is worshipped as the eighth avatar of Vishnu and also as the Supreme god in his own right. He is the god of protection, compassion, tenderness, and love; and is one of the most popular and widely revered among Indian divinities.[222]

There is that word compassion again.

It so happens...

222   Krishna. (2022). In *Wikipedia*. https://en.wikipedia.org/w/index.php?title=Krishna&oldid=1125677266

Buddha became a monk in the Hindu tradition and then he shared the path to monkhood with everybody. He never discarded the Gods or Goddesses. He put the Buddha (the enlightened) first, which was already how it was.[223]

Do you see how all these random, metaphysical visions I have seen in real life, in dreams, and under hypnosis fit together, perfectly, like a jigsaw puzzle? Even the date of my back operation (08-18-2021) digitally adds up to the Master Number twenty-two. With an understanding of what each puzzle piece means, I can fit together all of the puzzle pieces I have collected through the years, and in doing so, discover a grand picture of reality extending beyond our physical realm.

I certainly did not plan to be operated on by a doctor with the last name of Krishna, on 08-18-2021, and recover in a rental home with a giant picture of the Buddha on the wall. Buddha easily fits into the definition of an ascended master ready to help you on your journey through life.

In the bedroom of the rental home, there was a medium-sized oil painting of a somewhat abstract, dark, blue-faced figure. It might have been a painting of an ancient Aztec shaman. What immediately came to my mind was an Indigo child because of the painting's unique, dark blue (indigo) colored face.

For me, the two paintings in the Phoenix, AZ rental exuded powerful wisdom and healing energy. I felt safe and secure in

---

223   *Is Buddhism a Part of Hinduism.* (n.d.). Art Of Living (Global). Retrieved December 25, 2022, from https://www.artofliving.org/wisdom/theme/is-Buddhism-part-of-Hinduism

the calming and healing environment of the rental house while I healed after very invasive surgery. I needed all the help I could get to heal quickly. The pain was extraordinary, post-surgery, due to all the hardware being placed in such a small, sensitive area of my lower spinal cord. Looking back now, it was worth the very long recovery. The extreme, lower back pain I was experiencing before the surgery had become unbearable.

On another visit to Phoenix, I rented a home and noticed the following message displayed in a small, modest picture frame.

NEVER GIVE UP
No matter what is going on
Never give up
Develop the heart
Too much energy in your country
Is spent developing the mind
Instead of the heart
Be compassionate
Not just to your friends
But to everyone
Be compassionate
Work for peace
In your heart and in the world
Work for peace
And I say again
Never give up
No matter what is going on around you
Never give up

— Dalai Lama XIV [224]

These wise words were written by the fourteenth Dalai Lama.

---

224   *A quote by Dalai Lama XIV.* (n.d.). Retrieved December 29, 2022, from https://www.goodreads.com/quotes/168851-never-give-up-no-matter-what-is-going-on-never

Although I still seem to act like a bit of a pest in many of the otherworldly dreams I have, I feel like I have slowly progressed in my soul's self-actualization process. In this life, I did not take the easy way out.[225] There seems to be a great spiritually guided effort, via my dreams and the QHHT visions, to make me more aware of the whole afterlife process and the unrelenting love and compassion emanating from the spirit world. I chose to listen and learn. I am often reminded by my spiritual guides to never give up. They did not give up on me.

Spiritual understanding and compassion are key themes in many of my afterlife visions and dreams. Through these strange visions, I was shown how, by practicing acts of compassion, I can be promoted to a higher level of consciousness on the other side.

I wanted this book to be an honest account of the metaphysical knowledge I have gained in a short time and the profound, spiritually enlightened journey of discovery I went on. I learned a lot about who I am, spiritually, and what is important for me to do in this life. I quoted reputable, intelligent authors. After extensive research, I found convincing definitions and explanations of my spiritual dreams and visions. I have shown there is ample evidence of a greater, eternal, spiritual meaning to life and very convincing evidence of an afterlife.

I am not a very emotional person but when research guides me to a spiritual conclusion, I am, now, more open to sharing my

---

225   Major, M. 'I Took the Easy Way Out!', *Religion of One*, (05-15-2018). https://relofone.blogspot.com/2018/05/05-15-2018-i-took-easy-way-out.html

emotional, spiritual lessons with others. It does not bother me if someone else has a different opinion. We are all on a unique journey in this world and interpret things based on the tools we were born with or learn.

Self-actualization in all human beings is defined as the top tier in the pyramid-shaped hierarchy of needs defined in Maslow's Theory of Self-Actualization.[226] Each person on Earth must first master the physiological, psychological, and social needs at the lowest level of the pyramid, ascend to the next tier in the pyramid, and finally obtain the ultimate fulfillment in terms of life's meaning.

The visions of pyramids in my QHHT session showed me how our souls are reincarnated back to Earth. These pyramids were a key part of the iterative process of reincarnation to purge all of the karmic baggage I had accumulated from one life to another with the ultimate goal of being one with God.

Maslow's pyramid-shaped ascension could also be used to define a path to achieving a higher spiritual level of consciousness. If you listen to the voices within you and open up to truly understanding the metaphysical visions and dreams you have, a path to a higher level of spiritual self-actualization will open up to you.

My spirit guides will help me achieve a higher level of spiritual self-actualization. I am convinced of this. It is interesting to note

226   *What is Maslow's Hierarchy of Needs: Know What You Really Want.* (2020, May 30). Calm Sage - Your Guide to Mental and Emotional Well-Being. https://www.calmsage.com/understand-maslows-hierarchy-of-needs/

many people believe we have entered the Age of Aquarius— the *Age of Being*.

Maslow's highest level of self-actualization is…

being needs, indicated by the need for creative self-development in terms of one's potential toward a goal and a sense of meaning in life.[227]

There is a greater meaning to *being* than fulfilling your self-actualization needs on an Earthly plane of existence. I have learned it is possible to discover your current soul's mission on Earth and gain a broader view of your eternal Higher Self's intentions at a higher spiritual plane of existence.

I now know there is a greater spiritual meaning to life. Ultimately, you will no longer have to reincarnate back to Earth and fulfill more soul contracts because your soul has reached the highest vibrational plane possible on Earth.

To spiritually progress, I need to practice showing more compassion in this life. I must follow the will of my Higher Self, instead of following the path of being the rebellious soul I was in several previous reincarnations.

[The Buddhist concept of …] *Karma translates to action and the idea keeps us on a more mindful path, knowing that whether we give out good energy or bad, the law of cause and effect will balance this*

227   PsyD, A. R. (2013, January 8). *Maslow's Theory of Self-Actualization, More or Less Actualized.* https://brainblog-ger.com/2013/01/08/maslows-theory-of-self-actualiza-tion-more-or-less-actualized/

energy and it will eventually be returned to us.[228]

There could not be a clearer message for me to follow than what my Higher Self said during my pre-QHHT cleansing session,

I am standing in my power. I am evolving. I am compassion.

I thought I would see a bunch of dead relatives during my QHHT session. I guess I did, in a way. I found out I am in the same soul family as Archangel Metatron. Archangel Metatron could be considered a relative of mine.

Yet, in my newly found, superconscious mind's eye, Archangel Metatron is not dead.

Archangel Metatron is very much alive.

He will continue to help guide me toward a higher level of compassion and spiritual self-actualization.

Who is your spirit guide?

228   'Ashley, K. (2019, December 3). 5 Reasons Why You're Stuck In Bad Karma (and how to get free of it). *Spiritual Awakening Signs.* https://spiritualawakeningsigns.com/spiritualawakening/5-reasons-why-youre-stuck-in-bad-karma-and-how-to-get-free-of-it/

Appendix I

Here are selected examples of some of the strange afterlife dreams I have blogged about. They are in chronological order. Notice the emphasis on color and the highly structured afterlife environment I seemed to blatantly rebel against in my dreams. I was truly a rebellious soul or perhaps, a kinder way of putting it is …

Even in my afterlife dreams, I have always been a free spirit.

02/18/2014 NEXT GADGET RAGE?

I had a dream before I woke up this morning (02/18/2014). The dream was about a wristband made of what appeared to be semi-transparent, plastic or fused glass beads. It changed color when it sensed someone was invading your personal space. There were variations of the color-changing beads. The ones I saw worn in my dream changed to purple, green, or a varied pattern of purple and green. Memorable and nothing I ever think about so I believe it is a prediction of some item or event I will see in the future. I might do an internet search on the green or purple color-changing beads to see if I get a hit.[229]

---

229   Major, M. 'Next Gadget Rage?', *Religion of One* (02-18-2014). https://relofone.blogspot.com/2014/02/02182014-next-gadget-rage.html

The 'Next Gadget Rage' dream was over six years before I knew anything about Michael Newton's highly structured existence of souls in the afterlife where he discovered color defined the level of advancement a soul had progressed toward being one with God. I started noticing several dreams where I stressed the importance of specific colors.

11/24/2014 THANK YOU ANGEL WITH THE RED DRESS ON!

… The 11/24/2014 dream was with a different entity. It was a flashy young girl of about 25 or so. She was in a short, vibrant red dress…. definitely your aggressive, Type A personality.

She said she was sent down from above to help guide me, but what she really wanted to do was to get in a hot car and drive with the pedal to the metal on a long, winding road.

I tell you right now, this isn't me talking…

Anyway, we got in a car in my dream and started driving. The dream morphed into driving to visit my mother. On the way, we stopped at a gas station and, to my surprise, John Lennon was playing an impromptu concert there. I thought the concert in my dream was cool but, as you know, John Lennon is no longer with us in real life.

So, we drove on for a while and it seemed like a frivolous way to spend my time, so I asked her what this was all about since my mom already had passed away, as well.

She said something funny and I laughed.

Then she said,

'All I wanted to really do was see you smile.'

She was genuinely sweet. Brings a tear to my eye.

*Apparently, I haven't been smiling enough lately. I know
I have been too concerned with unimportant things in the
past few days.*

Thank you Angel with the Red Dress On!

*On the night of 11/25/2014, I had a dream I can't remember
too well.*

*What stood out was that I was excited about seeing
something and called my wife to come and take a look.*

*She was holding a baby in her arms. We are now too old to
have kids. Maybe this is a glimpse at a future grandchild.*
:-)[230]

I just noticed the exact day and month of my granddaughter's
birth can easily be derived from the date of the night I had the
11-25-2014 dream.

I also noticed my guardian angel with the red dress on missed
the physical thrill of driving with the pedal to the metal on a
long, winding road. Some souls miss certain physical sensations
they experienced while on Earth.

230   Major, M. 'Thank you Angel with the Red Dress
On!', *Religion of One* (11-24-2014). https://relofone.blogspot.
com/2014/11/11242014-thank-you-angel-with-red-dress.html

Yes, the vision of my wife holding a baby was a premonition. I am the proud grandpa of two girls. The real-life event occurred five years after I had that dream. The first was born in the same month I had the vision of my wife holding a baby.

03−20−2017 DO A SPIN FOR ME

So now I'm in this bare room being interviewed for various roles in a play. There are specific video recordings of each different role. I reviewed a few of the video recordings and told this entity, who took over my dream, that I did not feel this was my thing. I did not fit any of the roles they needed.

I get a very close-up image of the entity's long, manicured fingernails. Her fingernails were painted a light shade of purple with a broad stripe of a darker shade of purple painted in the center of the fingernail. Inside the broad stripe of darker purple was a very thin line of yellow ochre-colored nail polish.

Bizarre!

Right after the image of the entity's fingernails, the entity responded to my statement about not fitting any role they wanted by saying, 'Do a spin for me'.

The spin the entity requested turned me into a swirling mass of colors. My swirling image was an almost cylindrical funnel of short, curved, thin lines of color swirling around a black hole funnel. It was as if I was given a view of what a person would look like if they were caught in a black hole and shredded to bits — literally bits of color.

My subconscious mind seemed to be telling me,

'This is what you look like at the end of a black hole near the point of singularity. A swirling cylinder of short, thin, curved lines of different shades of colors.'

I noticed my spin had a lot of short bursts of purple and yellow ochre in the swirling cylinder of colors.

My spin had revealed my true colors.

My conscious mind immediately compared the swirling cylinder of short colored bursts to a phonograph record. It was telling me the short bursts of color could be translated into an entity just like the grooves in a phonograph record could be translated into a song.

I think this dream is very significant.

It is trying to tell me what we look like on the other side — after death where your true colors are revealed.

Wow!

This is the first time I have ever had such a clear image of what we may look like when we leave our bodies and enter another dimension where time and space become one...[231]

231   Major, M. 'Do a Spin for Me', Religion of One (03-20-2017). https://relofone.blogspot.com/2017/03/03-20-2017-do-spin-for-me.html

David Allen Hulse writes, in his article, 'Michael Newton's Color Scale of the Soul's Evolution and the Five Medicine Buddhas of Tibet,':

In his second book, Destiny of Souls[232], a table of color correspondences for the soul is shown in chapter five. On page 171 Dr. Newton has given us a table to show the various gradations of color marking the soul's evolution. 'Figure 6: Color Spectrum of Spiritual Auras' gives the following general ranking of the soul via color. Dr. Newton has premised six grades of spiritual evolution for the soul based on the 'soul's primary core colors.' The lowest grade (Level 1) is that of a beginning soul, while the highest grade in his system (Level 6) is that of an 'ascended master'.

Here is the basic color symbolism of this soul classification system. There is an overlapping of colors between grades, but the table below shows the primary colors associated with each of these six levels of soul evolution:

Color/ Level/ Grade

White/ 1/ Beginning Soul

Red/ 2/ Advancing Soul

Yellow/ 3/ Teacher

Green/ 4/ Healer

Blue/ 5/ Master

Blue Violet/ 6/ Ascended Master

Purple/ The Higher Levels/ Leading to the Godhead

232   Destiny of Souls. (n.d.). Retrieved December 18, 2022, from https://www.newtoninstitute.org/publication/destiny-of-souls/

... But in the scale of the soul's evolution, white is not the ultimate color of perfection, but rather the color of the innocent beginnings of the soul. It is the soul's color in its pristine state of inception, but not its final evolutionary hue.

The rainbow is stretched from the lowest vibratory rate of red to its highest vibratory rate of ultraviolet. Here red symbolizes the first hue of the rainbow that the soul radiates as a beginner on the spiritual path.

Violet represents the highest vibratory level of the soul that Newton was able to chart. Levels 1 through 5 are progressive points of the soul's evolution while still acquiring a physical body through the process of reincarnation. Level 6 and beyond represents the soul no longer requiring a physical incarnation to further develop the soul. So, Level 5, which is associated with deep blue, is the last aura change that the soul acquires while still using a physical body to further evolve along spiritual lines.

In the Golden Dawn[233] tradition of ritual magic, the use of the rainbow as a rich source of symbolism is deeply woven into the teachings of this esoteric magical order. The rainbow is stretched over the body as twelve gradations of color, with red at the head symbolizing the zodiac sign of Aries while red violet at the opposite end of the spectrum is associated with the feet and the zodiac sign of Pisces. Here the aura of the body is twelve-toned with red at the top and red-violet at the bottom.

233   Greer, I. R., John Michael. (2016). *The Golden Dawn.* https://www.llewellyn.com/product.php?ean=9780738743998

In modern chakra systems, the symbolism of the colors of the spectrum is reversed from the astrological symbolism of color in the Golden Dawn. Here the lowest chakra at the base of the spine is associated with the color red while the other six higher chakras become the rainbow scale of orange, yellow, green, blue, and blue-violet, ending in violet (at the crown of the head). This rise of spiritual energy (kundalini) through the chakras moves up the rainbow from red to violet. This rise of energy neatly parallels the levels of the souls as charted out by Dr. Newton.[234]

When you enter the afterlife, you go through a review of your previous life on Earth.

The color of a soul's aura is based on how old and what level of knowledge your soul is at and what you have accomplished in your current life on Earth.

05−15−2018 I TOOK THE EASY WAY OUT!

I had a strange, memorable dream in the early morning of 05-15-2018. It is kind of personal and I feel vulnerable blogging about it, but there are some interesting hints regarding what life after death might be like.

In the dream, I was walking in front of a large crowd of people in a stadium. The crowd was sitting in bleacher

234   Hulse, D. A. (2009, June 1). Michael Newton's Color Scale of the Soul's Evolution and the Five Medicine Buddhas of Tibet. Llewellyn Worldwide. https://www.llewellyn.com/journal/article/1855.

seats to the right of the front aisle I was walking down. All of a sudden, I heard someone shout out, 'You took the easy way out!' I felt caught off guard and singled out from the crowd. I kept walking and immediately pointed to my head as if saying, 'Because I was smart.'

The next scene in the dream jumped to an image of me sitting far up in the 'nosebleed' section of the stadium in the farthest corner, away from the crowd. I felt squeezed between too many people, so I moved even closer to the corner of the upper portion of the stadium to get more breathing room.

The scene in my dream then morphed into me staring down onto the field of the stadium at a row of people sitting behind a long table, looking up at the spectators in the stands. They appeared to me to be judges. I looked at each person behind the long table to try and figure out who yelled at me when I was walking by (in front of them) to get to my stadium seat. There were two men with light purple faces and strong, facial bone structures I immediately recognized as the people telling me I took the easy way out.

I felt this table of judges was there to assess me after my death. This judgment affected how I would be treated after death.

I was feeling claustrophobic and seemed to have a head cold, so I decided to leave the stadium event early.

As I was leaving the event, a slight, nerdy-looking man

with longer bleached blond hair, wearing glasses and a red with white polka dot shirt, asked me, 'Leaving so soon?' He seemed to genuinely care about how I was feeling.

I said, 'I have a cold and my pants are falling down.' I looked down at my pants and my zipper was open and I had two belts on instead of one. People passing me in the crowd started to snicker. I felt like a total social misfit but didn't seem to care very much.

'It was just the way it is,' I said to myself.

I have to admit I am slipping a bit in my proper dress code as I get older but never really felt I was a total misfit like this dream showed.

What I find interesting in this dream are two things.

1) The two twins with light purple faces and strong, facial bone structures who I felt were the ones who judged me were aliens – not from planet Earth. Have you ever wondered if alien life exists in the 'afterlife'? Well, now you know. There are aliens with purple faces and strong, facial bone structures on the other side, possibly even judging the life you led when you were alive...according to my dream.

2) The bleach blond-haired guy with a red and white polka dot shirt in my dream appeared to me to be another one of my 'guardian angels'. He seemed kind and genuinely caring about how I was feeling. What is significant about this guardian angel is he appeared in a red outfit, just like

the female guardian angel I had a dream about a long time ago.[235]

The people in my dreams dressed in red are most likely my guardian angels, and there are aliens, along with people from the Earth, in the afterlife. Good to know.

07–07–2018 I AM BECOMING A BIT OF A PEST IN OTHER WORLDLY DREAMS

It must be 'other world' week. I had two more dreams last night where I was floating around looking into people's private quarters... The first dream was a spin-off of the teenage kid's novel I am reading: <u>The Kane Chronicles, Book One: The Red Pyramid</u> by Rick Riordan.

In my dream, I was in this evil entity's house. In the book, it was the dwelling of Set – an evil god.

I was in a cluttered living room with a small secretary's desk, lots of random books, a couple of overstuffed chairs, a small puppy, and a small kitten. The kitten was wildly chasing its own tail around and around. There was also a woman, probably in her sixties with medium-length, greying hair seated at the secretary's desk busily writing in a book.

I had come into the room after exploring the second story

235   Major, M. 'Thank you Angel with the Red Dress On!', Religion of One (11-24-2014). https://relofone.blogspot.com/2014/11/11242014-thank-you-angel-with-red-dress.html

of the house and deciding the room I was in was some sort of prison. I managed to float out of the room, down to the first floor, and into the living room.

I started talking to the lady behind the secretary's desk, telling her I had been exploring a prison room on the second floor. Without looking up at me, the lady said, 'Set won't like it that you are here.'

I started waking up from my dream and heard a loud evil voice. The voice seemed to take over my whole consciousness like an emergency test screen on a regularly scheduled TV program. The loud evil voice said, 'Go Home!'

I have never experienced such a powerful, clear voice before in a dream. It shook me to my core. I was even more shocked by the voice because I had already started to wake up from my dream. I felt I had violated some evil entity's sanctum and in no uncertain terms should I ever do it again.

Then I drifted off to sleep again and had another dream where I was looking over a conversation in text, like a running phone text message. It was someone critiquing something I had written. Then it switched to a Japanese phone text I couldn't read. There was a lean-looking, greying Japanese man reviewing the cell phone text messages. I floated over next to him and asked him what it said. He indicated it was a conversation regarding a lady commenting on some picture of an ancient, handsome, Japanese prince. She kept saying, according to the man's interpretation, 'Oh, he is nice looking, really nice.'

Then the lean, greying Japanese man interpreting the text for me looked sideways at me. His eyes started to widen in surprise and fear. I think he was looking at something he didn't expect to see — like a ghost.

08-31-2018 MY JUDGEMENT DAY

I have had three dreams in the past three days that I remember as being odd. They were all related to each other. I have mentioned in the past I have dreams where I feel I am in another world observing a parallel universe or, perhaps, people on the other side.

The first dream, which I had a couple of days ago, was me being presented to a small group of adults by my old boss who died of brain cancer. He simply brought me into a small, darkly lit room and had me sit down. I suspect he is one of my guardian angels looking out for me on the other side.

I sit down and a lean, smartly-dressed, and stern-looking lady starts reading some notes as if she is evaluating my situation. I felt she wasn't too sure I was up to her standards.

Myself, I was obnoxious and free-spirited in the room. I was bragging about my relatives and how successful they were in life and talking a little too much. The lady evaluating me seemed irritated and rolled her eyes at me. The other people in the room seemed to be nervous for me like they wanted to tell me to keep quiet.

After a couple of minutes, the lady said, 'Alright, let's give him a task to do and see how he does.' I was handed some paperwork and ushered out the door with an assistant or two and sent on my merry way. I was still high-spirited and chatted aimlessly with the assistants while being ushered out of the area.

Weird! I have no idea what task was assigned to me. I forgot because I was talking too much in my dream.

The other two dreams were early this morning (08-31-2018). The first dream was a scene where I felt I had entered a different world and was lying on a bench in a men's locker room with red shorts on and a T-shirt. To my left were rows of adult men in their twenties – fit, well-disciplined men, in strict military postures. They were lined up in about six rows in an 'at ease' stance, staring at me. They had red shorts and T-shirts on too.

I said, nervously, 'This ain't Kansas!' One of the men in the rows cracked a half smile but immediately quit smiling as a leader entered the room and walked down in front of the bench toward me.

I was very nervous because I thought wearing red shorts meant I was in hell and this was the leader of a 'hell squad' I didn't want any part of. I told the leader, 'I wasn't feeling well' – after assessing the fact I was dressed just like the other men, except I was lazily lying down on a bench while *everyone else was at strict attention.*

The leader grinned and pronounced, Not feeling well, to everyone. He looked relaxed and was not mad at me at all. He was very kind to me. He said, 'Well, let's get you on your way.' This reaction from someone on the other side stands in stark contrast to people's reactions to my presence in previous otherworldly dreams. In past dreams like this, I was either ignored or I was aggressively attacked as being someone or something they did not want to have around.

In the otherworldly dream this morning, I felt the people were much nicer – selfless and kind in their interactions with me. It was very refreshing. I could relax around these people. Maybe the men in red shorts were angels in training. I was ushered out of the locker room, so I guess I'm not quite ready for the 'angels in training' process yet. I remembered that in a previous dream, a woman visited me in a red dress to try and get me to smile. There seems to be a theme going on here with red clothing and feel-good deeds from 'the other side'.

I had another dream a little later in the early morning. This time, there was a younger lady in her late teens talking to me about what her goal was 'on the other side'. She was so happy to see me and kept cupping her hands around my face under my chin as if she knew me. She said she wanted to make sure people were much more aware of the needs of people with mental health issues. She would dedicate her time to try to make sure people with mental health issues were treated fairly in life.

Again, I felt this person was genuinely selfless and caring. So much nicer than the previous people I met in my other dreams. It could be somebody I knew who died with mental health issues but is in a much healthier state now — unburdened by their physical illness.

In summary, although I still seem to act like a bit of a pest in otherworldly dreams, I felt I had been promoted to interact with more caring and loving people than in previous dreams.

I remember the 'Seatbelt Psychic', Thomas John[236], mentioning that there were different levels on the other side in one of his TV episodes, where the nicer people hung out together and seemed to have graduated further in their journey of self-actualization.[237]

Nice! I've been promoted on the other side...I hope.[238]

While proofreading this book on 07-09-2022, I realized the lady cupping my face with her hands and telling me she was so happy to see me was probably my half-sister Elaine in the

236   Seatbelt Psychic. (2022). In Wikipedia. https://en.wikipedia. org/w/index.php?title=Seatbelt_Psychic&oldid=1125428215.
237   PsyD, A. R. (2013, January 8). Maslow's Theory of Self-Actualization, More or Less Actualized. https://brain-blogger.com/2013/01/08/ maslows-theory-of-self-actualiza-tion-more-or-less-actualized/
238   Major, M. 'My Judgement Day', Religion of One (08-31-2018). https://relofone.blogspot.com/2018/08/08-31-2018-my-judgement-day.html

afterlife. She was severely mentally disabled in real life. It makes sense she wanted to dedicate her efforts in the afterlife to mental health issues.

10-25-2018 DREAM OF ASCENDING INTO HEAVEN BY AN ELEVATOR

Initially, I didn't want to post this because it is silly. I had a dream around 10-22-2018 where I was going up in an elevator. The elevator door opened and I saw several twenty-something adults chatting in small groups. Their dress was fairly colorful, but not gaudy. Color in the afterlife seems to be very important.

My initial thought of this dream was the feeling I had 'ascended' into heaven for a look around. I, again, immediately noticed how genuinely nice and non-threatening the people were.

A nice place to end up in the afterlife!

12-01-2018 I WOKE UP FROM A DREAM I HAVE HAD BEFORE AND IT IS STARTING TO FREAK ME OUT

I woke up from a dream on 12-01-2018. It was a strange dream and made me very uneasy. I was a resident in this dingy white multi-story apartment complex with shared entryways into each apartment. I was having trouble remembering which door was my apartment door. My mind was very scattered. I attributed it to my Attention Deficit Disorder. I was getting frustrated because I couldn't concentrate long enough on one thing to remember what floor I was on.

I ended up on the top floor of the building and there was a very large open-air restaurant and bar with over a thousand people lounging, listening to live music, and having drinks. I thought this was very nice and I should be taking advantage of this recreation space so close to my drab, sparse apartment. It was as if I was living a modest life in a rundown apartment and these people were above me, enjoying life and just relaxing.

Update 12-03-2018:

Thinking back on the image of the night sky in this dream at the open-air restaurant bar, I remember there were no stars in the night sky. None! Just pitch black. I'm going to miss the night sky with stars when I pass to the other side. :-(

I kept walking through the restaurant/bar and noticed there were another thousand people on another restaurant level, enjoying the evening outside. I walked past the singer playing the piano and noticed he was David Cassidy. I started freaking out because, in the back of my mind, I seem to remember David Cassidy passed away a while back.

David Cassidy was singing at the piano and he was not looking too good. His face was pale white and swollen.

As I started freaking out, I remember talking to myself in my dream, saying, 'What is going on with this dream? Why am I in a lousy, rundown apartment complex when I'm dead while thousands of other people are above me, partying all night long and having a good time? Is this my fate when I die?'

A kind voice answered back in my mind, 'You need to decide a job you want to do when you go to heaven.'

So, I said curtly, 'Fine, I want to be a guardian angel of babies and dogs.'

Then I woke up.

On the morning of December 2, 2018, I checked on the internet to see if David Cassidy had passed away. Yes, he had. He died from liver failure and admitted he was still drinking too much when he died. So maybe those thousands of dead people partying above me were not having a good time and died from drinking too much like David Cassidy? I guess the grass isn't always greener on the other side, even though it may appear so. :-)[239]

12−18−2018 A DREAM OF RECKONING

I had a memorable dream in the early morning of 12-18-2018. There were two scenes I remember distinctly in this dream.

---

239   Major, M. 'I Woke Up From A Dream I Have Had Before And It Is Starting To Freak Me Out', Religion of One (12-01-2018). https://relofone.blogspot.com/2018/12/12-01-2018-i-woke-up-from-dream-i-have.html

The first scene was a view of myself with some other apprentices pounding together at an angle a couple of greying 2 x 4 inch timbers over eight feet long, each using sturdy, round-headed four-inch steel nails. A tall, medium-set supervisor came along and showed us an example of how to properly nail two lengths of board together at a right angle. He made sure the other apprentices were able to see the proper nail pattern while he crowded me out of the way. The supervisor started walking away and I ran after him. I started to walk at his quick pace and politely asked him if I could have a closer look at the nail pattern so I could get it right in the future. He didn't stop walking but showed me the nail pattern of the sample, an angled piece of wood he was carrying.

I examined the nail pattern used closely. There were four nails lined up at the seam connecting the two angled pieces of wood together. I only saw the flush nail heads in the wood. I assume the nails were angled between the two pieces of wood at the seam – otherwise, it would not secure the two pieces of wood together. The pattern was very significant, one large, gold nail with a square head and then three round-headed, gold nails beneath the square-headed nail in a straight line.

Sometimes in these dreams, I am totally ignored or treated nicely by other entities in the dream. Not in this one. The tall, overbearing supervisor showed me the nail head pattern but then proceeded to yell at me and tell me in no uncertain terms he did not want me working with him, ever. He told me I have a history of being brash, rude, and judgmental at times when other people are at their weakest points emotionally. Basically, he told me to get lost – and for good.

Very disturbing. I didn't like the supervisor in my dream.

In the next scene, I was flying around this parallel world in what looked like a cushy, form-fitting seat from a chair without any chair legs or chair back. I was floating around this business district of a city at night with minimal lighting and somehow found myself in a very large auditorium-style room with seats angling down to the center stage. I was traveling a little too fast and twisted around so my back was to the stage and far wall. I was about to careen into the wall. I tried desperately to slow down and stop before hitting it. During this maneuver, I heard a man I passed telling me to be more careful and stop flying around the city without first looking at a map and determining the exact location of where I wanted to go. As if he was speaking to someone else, he said, 'He is so careless. He always zips around without really knowing where he is going. He is very reckless.'

Ha! I tell you it was a dream of reckoning. I felt like I was being judged again by otherworldly figures. I have had two or three other dreams like this recently.

Of course, my feelings after the dream were defiant and, in my mind, I said, 'Screw you!' A typical response my sometimes rude and sometimes vicious subconscious mind would say.

I think there is a symbolic meaning behind the one square-headed nail (a very old, handmade style of the nail) and the three round-headed (more modern, machine-made) types of nails in a straight-line pattern at the apex of a right-angled seam of wood.

So, my mind starts racing with ideas...

One part old, three parts new... apex fastened by golden nails in a pattern... parallel worlds...

I came up with the idea that maybe my dream is trying to tell me parallel worlds are connected at an apex of dense, gold material and jet out at right angles to each other from this dense apex. I picture in my mind lots of right-angled parallel worlds jetting out from a dense 'pin cushion' center of gold material — not unlike the central dense singularity proposed to be at the depths of black holes. According to this model, there could be several parallel worlds at right angles to each other, fastened at the center by dense, gold material consisting of one part old, recycled universe material; and three parts new universe material. This is a model of parallel universes unlike any other I have ever heard about.[240]

---

240   Major, M. 'A Dream Of Reckoning', Religion of One (12-18-2018). https://relofone.blogspot.com/2018/12/12-18-2018-dream-of-reckoning.html

About the Author

Marcas Major is a self-published author. He uses his diverse set of skills and education to review controversial topics such as paranormal phenomena and the path toward spiritual enlightenment.

He was born in a small mining town in British Columbia, Canada. His family moved to the United States where Marcas went on to get a Bachelor of Science degree in Fisheries Management and a Master of Business (MBA) in Finance. His career pushed him to learn new computer technologies and apply his broad business and science education to analyze and convert old, manual business processes into computerized processes.

Marcas Major is a pseudonym used for his more controversial publications. He has also published Tickles the Bear children's books under his real name, Marcel Pighin.

Marcas is now retired and living in Bend, OR near family and friends. He enjoys hiking, traveling, and painting portraits and landscapes using oil, acrylic, and watercolor mediums.

Thank you for joining me on my journey.

marcasmajor.com

$24.99

ISBN 978-0-9841360-7-0

52499>

9 780984 136070

www.ingramcontent.com/pod-product-compliance
Lightning Source LLC
Chambersburg PA
CBHW070824100426

42813CB00003B/473